The
TAO TE CHING
(the one & only true translation)

Next to
THE HOLY BIBLE

Interpreted By:
The Anonymous Daughter-In-Law

For My Mother-in-law

CONTENTS

Introduction..VII

The Letter To My Mother-in-law................................1

A Word From Me (The Daughter-in-law).................25

The Response From My Mother-in-law...................36

The Transcribed Translation of the 'Tao Te Ching of Lao Tzu' next to 'The Holy Bible'.........................40

The Scientific Method of Transcribing
With Illustration..205

Resources and Recommended Reading..............211

INTRODUCTION

One sunny summer afternoon, my husband and I had his parents over to the house for lunch. We grilled burgers and sat on the screen porch chatting about the good ol' days as the ceiling fans lessened the heat of the day. At some point, the conversation turned to religion, and my husband's parents dropped a bomb on us. My husband's father said that he was a "Deist", and his mother said that she was a "Taoist". This information was shocking to my husband (and myself). He had always assumed that his parents were believers in the Bible and in Christ Jesus. After all, they were the ones who had raised him and his brother as "Christians". The family had always attended Church, as well as celebrated Christmas and Easter together. His parents had even taught him and his brother the Ten Commandments when they were just boys.

My husband and I knew Deists to believe in a god who does not interact with its/his/her creation, but we weren't familiar with Taoism. His mother tried to explain the 'Tao' to us, but when his parents left, we jumped on Google. Almost immediately, we realized that understanding this religious philosophy would take more than a quick Google search, and due to my husband's busy work schedule, that meant I had some extra homework. As a part time-student, I had the time available to read up on Taoism. So I ordered some books from Amazon and set myself to learning. After I had completed my inquiry, I wrote a letter to my mother-in-law in order to share everything I had discovered.

This book is that letter. My husband and I hope that by sharing our story, we can help others to understand the Taoist philosophy, as it compares to Biblical reality.

The Letter To My Mother-in-law

THE LETTER TO MY MOTHER-IN-LAW

Dear ███████,

Recently, you mentioned that you were taking a remote study course that was an overview of all the (major) religions of the world. Jokingly, I asked if you had decided on one for yourself yet, and you answered, "Yes. I prefer the Eastern philosophy of Taoism".

Well, this news was quite a surprise! I had always assumed that you were a Christian. I made this assumption because of the fact that you attend Church regularly, as well as celebrate Christmas and Easter. Making matters more confusing, I had never even heard of Taoism. If you'll recall, you had to explain that Taoism is the Eastern philosophy espousing that an unknown energy source created and sustains everything in the universe. You said, "the energy source is called 'Tao', for the lack of a better name and for the want of none". You pointed out that the absence of words to describe the Tao prevents it from being packaged into a religion with labels, names, sects, and deadly crusades. You recommended that if I wanted more insight into Taoism, I should read a book called, "Tao Te Ching of Lao Tzu". (Pronounced: Dao De Jing)

Well, I did want to know more and I'm writing you now to share the results of my inquiry, which became quite a journey! I have to admit, I didn't think there would be much to learn about a belief without established fundamentals - or even names - and now I feel like I know too much! What I've discovered could make "the powers that be" very angry; so if anything happens to me, please give this letter to my pastor. I guess I'll start at the beginning and tell you everything...

My journey began when I went on Amazon.com to buy the book you recommended. There were many versions of 'Tao Te Ching of Lao Tzu' to choose from. I assumed that was similar to the many translations of the Bible, so I ordered a few different versions thinking I could cross-reference them, if needed. When the books arrived, I read the eighty-one short chapters of each version, and unfortunately, I ended up with more questions than answers. For one thing, I didn't understand how the different versions could vary so much in content, being that they all originated from one source (or so I thought). To get answers, I decided to find and read the original translation of the original text.

That's when things got strange. I discovered that the original Chinese text is virtually unintelligible! As in, impossible to understand, or inscrutable. I found out that the Chinese don't even know its meaning! The ancient text is written in "classical" Chinese, which is different from modern Chinese writing. Classical Chinese contains characters that are more like pictures than words. This means the 'Tao Te Ching' is more like art or pictography, rather than literature. According to Wikipedia (under 'Tao Te Ching'), translating is made even more difficult because many of the characters are vague and ambiguous so as to only indirectly reference objects and circumstances.

Needless to say, my search for an original translation was over. The word "translation" means converting text from one language to another. Now I had learned that every translation is instead, an interpretation, which is a stylistic explanation of a creative work. This means that all interpretations have a meaning specifically significant to the interpreter. The fact that the Chinese characters have no specific meaning explained the many differences in the interpretations, but it now posed a new question. How was it possible for the many different interpretations to promote a similar ideology without a common source of reference? I was stumped. That is, until I learned of the "Word Range Translation". This is what a Chinese translator creates when interpreting each individual Chinese character into several word possibilities. With a Word Range Translation, the Taoist interpreter has a word buffet to choose from for incorporation into his or her own interpretation of the 'Tao Te Ching'. As the word "interpretation" suggests, every interpreter is free to modify words in the Word Range Translation, and/or to add words into his or her final text, according to personal concepts.

THE LETTER TO MY MOTHER-IN-LAW

In addition to the Word Range Translation, I realized that there was another useful commonality among the many different interpretations-- it was their introduction pages! Many of the interpretations begin with an introduction that tells the story of the original author. As you may already know, they all say the true author is unknown; however, there is a legend. They go on to tell the legend of a man named, Li Er. (I thought the phonetic pronunciation of his name was interesting.)

As the legend goes, King Wu of Zhou appointed Li Er as head librarian of the royal archives at Luoyang. In this capacity, he was able to immerse himself in the study of history, philosophy and literature, gaining wisdom and insights along the way. According to legend, Confucius visited with Li Er and came away in awe of his intellect. Confucius recognized that Li Er had a deep understanding about the world - even superior to his own - and went so far as to liken Li Er to a mysterious dragon. (I thought the comparison to a dragon was also interesting.)

It is said that Li Er decided to leave civilization behind when the House of Zhao began its decline, so he departed Luoyang and headed through the Hangu Pass toward some destination beyond the Great Wall. Before leaving the gate at the Great Wall, Li Er was asked by the commander at the gate to write down his thoughts of wisdom for posterity. Li Er agreed, and wrote a small book expressing his accumulated learnings for the benefit of future ruler-sages. His focus was on achieving a good society through harmony with nature.

So, now I understood where both the differences and the similarities were coming from. The 'Tao Te Ching' is a personalized interpretation created from a Word Range Translation (i.e., a list of word possibilities pertaining to each Chinese character), and both are created with the incorporated ideas about the life and beliefs of a well-rounded, politically and socially-minded naturalist, who was a wise librarian during the Zhao dynasty around 500-200 B.C.

This style of interpretation is called "contextualism", and it would seem to be the only way that pictography could contribute to religious thought. That being said, it's my understanding that Taoists believe there are two categories of Taoism: secular and religious. This fact is very revealing because, as you know, the law of noncontradiction states that something cannot be true and untrue at the same time. The idea that natural creation and supernatural creation are both embraced within Taoism, reveals the true objective of Taoism. If belief in truth is not the objective, then belief in no truth becomes the objective. Secularism is the deliberate effort to be free of spirituality and religion, while religion is the deliberate effort to seek and embrace spiritual reality. These are two contradicting views that embrace contradicting creation theories. Thus, they preclude unification into one belief system. The choice between secular and religious Taoism is a reference to the true choice that exists --which is to believe man (secular), or to believe God (religious). However, within Taoism, both choices are a choice of unbelief because one is the choice of no god, and the other is the choice of a non-god (un-named and un-known).

The Bible provides evidence of one absolute truth, One Creator and Savior; and it says that we are His creation. The Bible says that a rejection of God's Word is the acceptance of humanism (secularism), as it puts the thoughts of man above divine reality without regard for Truth. There are many man-made "religions" in the world, but **only God's Word** says that it can act as a Light to guide us (Psalm 119:105). The author and Christian apologist, C.S. Lewis, said: "I believe in Christianity as I believe that the sun has risen: not only because I see it, but because by it I see everything else".

To better understand how God's Word is "Light", consider the law given to Moses by God (Exodus 20:1-17). God gave the law to Moses, so that man would have God's standard of righteousness to compare with man's own standard. By comparison, man is able to see that his natural condition is far from being righteous (Romans 7:7). God's Word conveys Truth, and a comparison reveals reality (truth or deception) (2 Corinthians 4:6).

THE LETTER TO MY MOTHER-IN-LAW

With that in mind, I decided to demonstrate how God's Word can reveal reality pertaining to the 'Tao Te Ching'. I wanted to compare the tenets of Taoism, to the tenets of the Christian Faith. To do this, I created a side-by-side comparison of the two founding texts, placing the 'Tao Te Ching' on the left, and correlating verses from 'The Holy Bible' on the right. This comparison revealed the objectives of both texts, the intentions of their words, and the consequences of believing the message contained in each.

Now, you're probably wondering whose interpretation of the 'Tao Te Ching', was used for the comparison, right? Well, I didn't use an interpretation. Remember, an interpretation is created with much individualized imagination. If I were to use an interpretation, I would only be comparing the mind of one Taoist to God's Word. My comparison required a literal translation of the 'Tao Te Ching', which meant that I had to transcribe the words directly from a Word Range Translation. To "transcribe" meant that I could only use the words found in the Word Range Translation. By transcribing instead of interpreting, I effectively replaced the creative process with a literal translation of the Chinese characters.

As it turned out, this method was the key to decoding the true meaning of the 'Tao Te Ching'!

Next, I'm sure you're wondering how could a Word Range Translation be used to produce a literal translation, if each Word Range is also an interpretation? For that answer, I point to the words of the Taoist experts. The first expert I communicated with was Robert G. Henricks, Professor Emeritus of Religion at Dartmouth College. He taught a class on Taoism and has published his own interpretation of the 'Tao Te Ching'. Professor Henricks said that only someone who knows classical Chinese (as he does) can translate the Chinese Characters. Then I communicated with the operator of the Taoist website, CenterTao.org. His name is Carl Abbott, and he also has published his own interpretation of the 'Tao Te Ching'. Like Professor Henricks, Mr. Abbott also stated that only a person who knows Chinese can produce a Word Range Translation.

THE LETTER TO MY MOTHER-IN-LAW

I was glad to have both experts on record as qualified "translators", given the fact that I was using their translations/interpretations in order to identify the correct words to transcribe. You see, when I took a closer look at their translations/interpretations, I realized that the Word Ranges were actually replicas of one another, but with personalized modifications and additions. Each expert translation of an individual character would have some combination of identical words, synonyms, and/or dissimilar words. This fact makes it possible to identify where a particular translator/interpreter has deviated from the consensus translation for the sake of their own interpretation.

More importantly, it meant that the original author had conveyed an original thought, if not through the characters/art work, then certainly through an intellectual epidemic -- I'll come back to this later. So now, it was clear to me that in order to determine the literal and true translation of the Tao Te Ching, all I had to do was cross-reference several translations/interpretations -- identifying the matching words and eliminating the random words. The real beauty of this method is the fact that each expert has published their own translation/interpretation, making it easy to prove that the words in my literal translation are theirs (not mine), and that the words in my translation are also definitive (the experts agree).

So, to recap, I had discovered that the 'Tao Te Ching' was pictography and open for Taoist interpretation within the spectrum of a general consensus. The author is unknown, but a legend is promoted in his or her stead. Almost all interpretations point to the legend as if it were the "construction permit" for building one's own religion. The interpretations all claim to promote piety despite being founded on subjective realities.

The philosophy of Taoism reminded me of a verse in the Bible that says: "Beware lest any man spoil you through philosophy and vain deceit, after the tradition of men, after the rudiments of the world, and not after Christ" (Colossians 2:8).

THE LETTER TO MY MOTHER-IN-LAW

In considering who authored the 'Tao Te Ching', my mind flashed back to my classroom days, and to a legal course I once took. The lawyer teaching the class said, "The best way to find the truth is to look for the lies". I always thought that was odd, but his point was that if you find a lie, then you'll find a motive; and when you find the motive, then you'll find the perpetrator. Well, nothing about the 'Tao Te Ching' was founded in truth; and that revealed a motive, which, in turn, enabled me to identify the true author. The true author is a dragon named, Li Er!

He is not a mythical character. God's Word warns us to "beware" of his tactics. His real name is Lucifer, the great dragon, the devil, Satan, the ancient serpent, liar (Revelation 20:2). He is the father of lies (John 8:44). His motive is for you to believe his words - and not God's Words. Taoism is a spiritual attack, and your rejection of Truth is the objective. Li Er is very real, and Jesus battled him on the Mount of Temptation (Matthew 4:1-11). Peter called him, "a roaring lion seeking whom he may devour" (1 Peter 5:8). Paul warned us not to be ignorant of his schemes (2 Corinthians 2:11).

The Light of God's Word reveals Taoism to be just another scheme by Satan meant to rob you of your eternal inheritance and reward. Think about it. The first few sentences of Li Er's little book of wisdom say: "The Tao (creator) that can be told is not the eternal Tao. The name that can be named is not the eternal Name. The unnameable is eternally real. The Tao that can be understood is not the eternal Tao. Tao is beyond words. The way that can be known is the wrong constant way." (Pulled from various interpretations.) The 'Tao Te Ching', in just the first few sentences, says that words cannot describe the Creator. Thus, if you believe Li Er, the battle is over. Li Er wins. With just a few sentences comprised of words, Li Er has you believing that words are powerless. Now compare that to what the Bible has to say about the power of words:

"In the beginning was the Word, and the Word was with God, and the Word was God" (John 1:1).

"Life and death are in the power of the tongue, and those who love it will eat its fruit" (Proverbs 18:21).

THE LETTER TO MY MOTHER-IN-LAW

"But I tell you that everyone will have to give account on the day of judgment for every empty word they have spoken. **For by your words you will be justified, and by your words you will be condemned**" (Matthew 12:36-37).

Taoism exists only to sabotage your ability to know God, to understand His plan, to believe His Word, and to have a relationship with Him. This is achieved by making you believe that words are futile, understanding is unobtainable, and that beliefs are inconsequential. However, the opposite is true. God teaches us to use reason and logic in order to recognize the truth and avoid the pitfalls of untruth. God knows that logic will lead you to truth, and truth will lead you to Him. Jesus said, "If I do not the works of my Father, believe me not. But if I do, though ye believe not me, believe the works: that ye may know, and believe, that the Father is in Me, and I in Him" (John 10:37-38).

This was His effort to make you think about the logic behind your unbelief. He understands that a man can reject the words of a man, but what if that Man proves that He has command over every subatomic particle in the universe? What if that Man has the ability to heal the blind, deaf, and sick; resurrect the dead; has command over the wind and rain; and can walk on water, etc. His point is, if you still don't believe Him, then you're not just rejecting the words of a man, you're rejecting logic. How else could a man have supernatural power, if it were not given Him from a supernatural Source? Taoists make the choice to ignore logic and replace God in their hearts with a myth. It's the myth that man has power within; man creates his own morals; man controls his own destiny; and man is his own judge. Ironically, the serpent, Li Er, presents a myth that offers a belief in one's own self for those who would demythologize the Bible in order to reject the Truth.

God uses His Power and Authority to teach, love, and lead us; but He also uses it to judge and condemn the unbelieving and rebellious (Genesis 1:1- Revelation 22:21). Thus, if He allowed even one unbeliever into His Kingdom, He would make Himself a liar and owe

THE LETTER TO MY MOTHER-IN-LAW

a lot of condemned people an apology. This is why it's crucially important that you understand, the Bible says that you can't enter God's Kingdom just because you're a nice person. If you reject the truth of God's Word, and accept Li Er's words, then you simply can't take the critical next steps to secure your eternity with the Lord. If words are meaningless to know your Creator, how likely are you to do the following: "If you declare with your mouth, 'Jesus is Lord', and believe in your heart that God raised him from the dead, you will be saved" (Romans 10:9).

God's Word is a call to action! Luke 11:9-10 says, "And I say unto you, Ask, and it shall be given you; seek, and ye shall find; knock, and it shall be opened unto you. For every one that asketh receiveth; and he that seeketh findeth; and to him that knocketh it shall be opened." This means that if we desire to know truth, and then act on that desire using words of intention, we will find Him.

As you know, the leading ethical concept in Taoism is "wu-wei" (woo-wey), or "wei-wu-wei", which means "action without intent" and "action without action". This is a call to inaction, or a call to action without intent, which, if embraced, causes you to reject the only true way to salvation. The Lord requires us to act **with** intent by way of repenting for our sins, by rejecting our natural sin nature, and by actively replacing it with our original nature/His Nature, through a renewing of our mind. Acts 3:19 says, "Repent ye therefore, and be converted, that your sins may be blotted out, when the times of refreshing shall come from the presence of the Lord;". Ephesians 4:22 says, "You took off your former way of life, the old self that is corrupted by deceitful desires; you are being renewed in the spirit of your minds; you put on the new self, the one created according to God's likeness in righteousness and purity of the truth."

To be saved out of sin, we have to act with that intent for the purpose of receiving His redemption. Redemption is His way of reuniting us to Himself by redeeming us according to His righteousness (not our own).

Ephesians 1:7 says, "In Him we have redemption through His blood, the forgiveness of sins, in accordance with the riches of God's grace...".

Another Taoist teaching that is opposed to God's requirement, is the value of naturalism, or "the way of nature". The Taoist metaphor for naturalness is pu (pǔ), which means, "uncarved wood". This concept is presented as a way of remaining indifferent, unmoved, or unshaped by what is going on around you. Pu refers to the primordial state-of-being prior to the imprint of culture on an individual.
However, The Bible tells us that our "primordial" state is the innate fallen and sinful nature given us at the fall of Adam.

Romans 5:12 says, "Wherefore, as by one man sin entered into the world, and death by sin; and so death passed upon all men, for that all have sinned".
So, Taoism teaches that the imprint of culture on a person is responsible for sin (or the feeling of guilt), and thus, sin is not innate in man. If you believe that, you will not reject your sin nature in order to embrace God's righteous nature as your substitute. It's only when we come into the Light of God's Word that we realize our natural condition is fallen. That realization then becomes the point at which the law of noncontradiction establishes God and the Bible, as Truth. Jesus can not be virtuous and a liar at the same time. We can not say that we are corrupt (or that He is righteous) at the same time that we purport to have no standard by which to measure. If you believe in the forces of good and evil (or yin and yang), then you should also believe in the only doctrinal text that explains their existence from inception. C.S. Lewis said, "Either Jesus is who He says He is, or He was the greatest lunatic who ever lived!"
This is an either-or.
You recently told me that you "follow Jesus' teachings", but it's important to understand that if someone claims to follow the teachings of Jesus, while they don't believe He is God incarnate, then that person is actually claiming to follow a righteous liar, and lying

about following at the same time. Once we acknowledge that the Bible is the true Word of God, we acknowledge the reality that we are spirits with human bodies, not humans with spirituality (1 Corinthians 9:27; 15:54). This makes our battles in this life, entirely spiritual. Ephesians 6:12 says, "For our struggle is not against flesh and blood, but against the rulers, against the authorities, against the powers of this dark world and against the spiritual forces of evil in the heavenly realms."

We can know that Taoism is from a spiritual place of opposition to God because the principles and values of Taoism oppose God's teaching. Our victory is realized spiritually, starting with the discernment to know truth from untruth, and that ability begins with the intention of our hearts. Do we sincerely desire to know the truth? Intention is what informs our belief. For example, if there is substantial evidence for the argument of evolution and substantial evidence for the argument of creationism -- neither having concrete proof -- then the one you choose to believe represents your intention and not any conclusive reasoning. Hebrews 11:1 says, "Faith is the substance of things _hoped_ for and the evidence of things _not seen_".

Initially, where you place your faith boils down to what you hope is true. Do you hope God's Word is true and that He created man? Or do you hope man evolved on his own over millions of years?
Faith is needed for both beliefs, but faith is only needed to believe in the Lord initially, because, after accepting Christ, the evidence of His Truth is manifested in our lives. God makes Himself known to us. The unseen evidence becomes seen by way of His promises. Matthew 5:8 says, "Blessed are the pure in heart, for they will see God".

So, His Word teaches logic, provides the truth, requires that we accept Him in Faith, and makes many promises to believers. Then our faith becomes the evidence showing Him our intention to place our hope in Him, which enables Him to reveal Himself to us more and more, until we are walking in His Light with the full knowledge of Him at His coming (Ephesians 4:13).

Taoism requires a lot of faith, too. After all, don't you hope Li Er is telling you the truth and that you won't have to answer to a knowable God? If this is your hope, what evidence does Li Er offer to back his claim that the Creator is unknowable? Where are all the witnesses to his power and authority, making him trustworthy? Where are his fulfilled prophecies that prove He is all-knowing? Where are his miracles to demonstrate his power? Where is his effort to teach you logic so that you can think for yourself? Where is the evidence that he loves you and would never try to deceive you? Surely, Li Er doesn't think he can win your belief by offering zero evidence for his words? Especially not while God offers countless evidences and countless eyewitnesses!

The Bible uses powerful words to describe a loving Creator with a very big plan. If you intend to know the truth and you want to understand His plan, you need only ask, seek, and knock with a heart that hopes He will answer. He is a loving God, thus, He didn't just say, "I Am God", and then require us to worship Him for that reason. I'm paraphrasing here, but He said, "I Am God; however, you decide if I'm lovable". Then He set about teaching us and revealing Himself to us. He wants to win our love. Once we choose to believe, He shares everything with us. If we choose not to believe, we will suffer in eternity as a result of our choice, but that makes logical sense, too. Unbelief is the crime of murder and identity theft. It's the choice to stand as one with those who called Jesus a liar and killed Him. By your unbelief, you are calling God a liar so that you can decide truth and morality in order to become your own judge. It's the choice to believe your own feelings on the matter of truth --rather than truth. Free will is the ability to accept (or reject) Jesus; but it also serves to prevent another rebellion in God's future Kingdom by allowing for self-eliminating egos. Free will is the sieve that separates those who love truth from those who want to make up their own truth.

THE LETTER TO MY MOTHER-IN-LAW

Free will is also at the center of the coming prophesied seven years of "Tribulation" (Daniel 9:27), and the coming war called, "Armageddon" (Revelation 16:16). It will be those who chose to reject Christ, versus Christ and His Church. Currently, we are witnessing prophecy unfold before our very eyes. The sons of Ishmael are making videos of beheadings for all to see. The book of Revelation foretells that many believers will be beheaded for the Lord's sake during the Tribulation (Daniel 12:4; Revelation 20:4). As of now, beheadings are for all "infidels" of Islam, but soon they will be for those who refuse to worship the antiChrist.

The seven year Tribulation will begin with a peace treaty in the Middle East (Daniel 9:27). The US Secretary of State, John Kerry, is currently trying to broker a peace treaty in the Middle East. So, you see, all the battles around us are spiritual. Even Taoism acknowledges spiritual warfare, as is evidenced by the (false) sense of security and escape offered. Taoism teaches that if you know nothing, desire nothing, do nothing, and say nothing, then you will always take the path of least resistance and nothing will happen to you. However, by not standing for Truth, something has already happened to you. You've chosen to be on the wrong side of prophecy. The true test for salvation is our answer to this one question:

If someone had a knife to your throat and demanded that you deny Jesus is the Son of God, would you? Those who are murdered because they won't reject Truth, are called martyrs, and prophecy says that martyrdom will increase during the Tribulation.

Wisdom is fearing the One Who can destroy both body AND soul (Proverbs 9:10; Matthew 10:28). With a knife to your throat, your choice is not to live or die (your soul is eternal), the choice is to reject, or not to reject, Truth. The Lord puts life and death before us and tells us to choose life, and that starts with being willing to die in our carnal humanity, as He did for us. Choosing 'life' refers to Him, the Eternal Life. Our created human life is but a vapor -- a puff of air -- compared to eternity (James 4:14). The purpose of this created human experience, the purpose of this vapor, is for each of us to take the test and make a choice. Truth or no truth?

THE LETTER TO MY MOTHER-IN-LAW

The Bible says that if a person does not receive a love of the Truth now (when it's as obvious as it is), then God will send a delusion to ensure that they believe the lie presented by the antiChrist -when he is revealed (2 Thessalonians 2:1-12). If it weren't for the delusion, the Truth would certainly be obvious to those who once doubted the Bible, and He can't allow anyone to make a decision for Him that doesn't require faith. Without faith, nothing is required of your own intention. Your heart and mind must intend to choose Him over man-made belief systems.

I'm curious, are you familiar with how the title, 'Tao Te Ching of LaoTzu', translates? The word Tao means "way" (or the way), the word Te, means "power", Ching means "book", and Lao Tzu means, "old master". Put it together and you have:
"The Way Power Book of Old Master". The title suggests a mockery of God's powerful, "I AM The Way" Book called, The Bible. The "Old Master" is Li Er, the serpent, and his book is full of lies meant to lead you A-WAY from Truth. By your not holding to Truth, Li Er wins, and you make him your master and his way, your way (John 8:44; 1 John 2:22).

Chapter fifty-six of the 'Tao Te Ching' is just one example proving that the power belongs to the Old Master and not to the Taoist. It says something to the effect of, "those who know, don't speak, and those who don't know, speak". This means you're clever to keep your mouth shut and unwise if you speak up. Where's the power in that? The power is in making you believe it. The power belongs to the ancient serpent whom you serve with your obedient rejection of Truth. The power is in having you forfeit the only tool you have to resist Satan's lies: **The Word**. You are powerless without The Word of God as your armor... and the evidence for that is your adoption of Taoism (Ephesians 6:10-18).

Look, I'm not a fire and brimstone person when it comes to telling others about Christ, but I don't avoid the topic either. Hell is real,

THE LETTER TO MY MOTHER-IN-LAW

and while God created it for Satan, those who side with Satan by denying God's Son, will join him there (2 Thessalonians 1:6-9). If you've studied the Bible and you've decided to reject the Truth, then I have to tell you, your soul is in eternal jeopardy! It breaks my heart to think of what you're missing with your choice not to know the Lord now, but also to think of what you will miss in His Kingdom. You will not be reunited with your believing family members that have gone before you, and that means you will not meet your third child that was returned to the Lord prior to being born. I know it's a difficult subject, but I believe that child is waiting to meet you. God knits us together in the womb.
Psalm 139:13 says, "For you created my inmost being; you knit me together in my mother's womb". King David refers to his deceased infant son by saying, "But now that he is dead, why should I go on fasting? Can I bring him back again? I will go to him, but he will not return to me" (2 Samuel 12:23).

Your family doesn't want you to lose your eternal inheritance. These are not just "self-soothing" beliefs. None of us are Christians because we can't accept death or because we like the crusades and spiritual battles that have always existed. We are believers in Christ because He has proven Himself to be the Truth. We don't have some social need to worship names or labels -- or to make intellectual sacrifices to a made-up supreme being. The desire to know our Heavenly Father is innate in all of us. Even you. Why else would you want to believe in the energy source, Tao? Or in any higher power for that matter? You are aware of the void that exists within you. Ecclesiastes 3:11 says, "He has made everything beautiful in its time. <u>He has also set eternity in the human heart</u>; yet no one can fathom what God has done from beginning to end."

There are only two possible outcomes in this life. We can choose to trust in Jesus' payment for our sin, or we can choose to pay for our sins ourselves. John 3:18 says, "Whoever believes in Him is not condemned, but whoever does not believe stands condemned already, because they have not believed in the name of God's one and only Son." Those who go to hell are specifically those who do not believe in Jesus' name. To "believe" goes beyond a mental recognition of the truth. To believe in Christ for salvation requires a transfer of allegiance. We stop serving ourselves, we forsake our sin nature, and we begin to serve God with our heart, soul, mind, and strength (Mark 12:30). C. S. Lewis, said it this way, "There are only two kinds of people in the end: those who say to God, 'Thy will be done,' and those to whom God says in the end, 'Thy will be done'". God desires that every person spend eternity with Him. 2 Peter 3:9 says, "The Lord does not delay His promise, as some understand delay, but is patient with you, not wanting any to perish but all to come to repentance".

I know you've said that you consider the 'Tao' to be a reference to God, but it's important that you understand, there is only one God. The God of the Bible. The Bible has nineteen names for God and none of them are Tao. In addition, a belief in God does not mean you're a Christian, or that you're saved into God's Kingdom. James 2:19 says, "You believe that God is one. You do well; the demons also believe, and shudder." 1 John 4:2-3 says, "By this you know the Spirit of God: every spirit that confesses that Jesus Christ has come in the flesh is from God; and every spirit that does <u>not</u> confess Jesus is not from God; this is the spirit of the antichrist, of which you have heard that it is coming, and now it is already in the world".
Rejecting Jesus is no small offense, and the only way to know Him is to trust God's Word, the Bible; and the only way to trust the Bible is to believe that all scripture is God Breathed (2 Timothy 3:16). If you can't trust the Bible, you can't trust the Lord, and that means you can't be in His Church as His Bride for eternity. This life is the dating process for that marriage. He wants to know who among us will believe in Him, trust Him, serve and love Him, for richer or poorer, in sickness and in health, unto death.
It's also important that you understand, the transcribed translation of the 'Tao Te Ching' enclosed with this letter, is the one and only true "translation" in existence. My translation was not interpreted

through a myth, nor through human imagination. 1 Corinthians 2:13-14 says, "Now we have received, not the spirit of the world, but the spirit which is of God; that we might know the things that are freely given to us of God. Which things also we speak, not in the words which man's wisdom teacheth, but which the Holy Ghost teacheth; comparing spiritual things with spiritual. But the natural man receiveth not the things of the Spirit of God: for they are foolishness unto him: neither can he know them, because they are spiritually discerned."

All words have spiritual intent behind them and it's important for us to have discernment to know of which spirit they are. Hebrews 4:12 says, "For the word of God is alive and active. Sharper than any double-edged sword, it penetrates even to dividing soul and spirit, joints and marrow; it judges the thoughts and attitudes of the heart."

The 'Tao Te Ching' is nothing more than a spiritual attack on those who lack discernment due to an unbelief in, or ignorance of, God's Word. Taoism, and any other belief system that sets itself up against Christ, serves only to divide the sheep from the goats in the end. False religions enable a Just and Fair God to purify His future Kingdom, righteously. Those who have heard the Gospel of Jesus Christ, but prefer the philosophy presented by Li Er, the dragon, will most certainly "be without excuse" (Romans 1:20).

Believers in Heaven will mourn the absence of those who rejected Truth. Families will reunite with tears of joy, but also with tears of sadness and loss, as they grieve for the unbelieving family members. Perhaps, even grieving their own lack of effort to speak the truth to them when they had the chance.

This sorrow, I believe, is the reason for this scripture: "<u>And God shall wipe away all tears from their eyes</u>; and there shall be no more death, neither sorrow, nor crying, neither shall there be any more pain: for the former things are passed away" (Revelation 21:4).

THE LETTER TO MY MOTHER-IN-LAW

The transcribed translation proves that without man's imagination, a divine reality exists. The Bible is the only book in the world that claims to contain a Living Word with the Power and Authority to expose and defeat a lying enemy. The Light of God's Word has exposed the true meaning of the 'Tao Te Ching' and proven it to be a deception. No other "religion" in the world could do the same. The Bible has miraculously revealed the true author, the true purpose of the writing, and its true meaning -- all while Taoists continue to have no idea who wrote it, why, or what it means!

Only truth can reveal untruth. This is the true function of the yin yang principle. It's the observation of the contrast created by truth and untruth (Light and darkness), that points us to a divine reality, and it's our relationship with the Lord that reveals The Way, The Truth, and The Life (John 14:6). The process of a contrast, combined with a revelation of Power and Authority, is His method of teaching and leading us.

For example, take the historical allegory of Moses and his staff. Moses' staff was turned into a serpent to prove God's Power was with him, and then the Pharaoh's two wise-men also appeared to turn their staffs into serpents in an effort to prove that they had the same power -- only to watch as Moses' serpent ate their serpents. The serpents all seemed equal until the one with Authority destroyed the others. Religions can seem similar, until God's Word exposes them as false, destroying the illusion.

Scripture tells us that Satan can appear as an angel of light (2 Corinthians 11:14). His appearance has power so as to deceive even the Elect, if it were possible (Matthew 24:24). This is why we need **discernment** to know whose words are true words and whose words are lies. Man has three vulnerabilities that Satan tries to use in order to deceive us: lust of the flesh, lust of the eyes, and pride of life.

The serpent told Eve that when she ate from the forbidden fruit, she would be as a god. She saw that the tree was good for food (lust of the flesh), the fruit was delightful to look at (lust of the eyes), and that it was desirable to make one wise (pride of life).

She believed Satan's words over God's words warning her not to partake (Genesis 3:1-6).

Satan tried to tempt Jesus, too. Jesus had been fasting for forty days when Satan suggested that Jesus turn a rock into bread (lust of the flesh, lust of the eyes, and pride of life). Satan showed Jesus all the Kingdom's of the world in a moment and offered Jesus all their power and glory if He would worship him (lust of the flesh, lust of the eyes, and pride of life). Satan took Jesus to the top of the temple in Jerusalem and told Him to throw His Body off in order to test God's Word which says that the angels will protect God's Son (lust of the flesh, lust of the eyes, and pride of life). With Eve, Satan was able to cause her to doubt God's words and partake, but with Jesus, for every temptation Satan tried, Jesus said: "It is written..."! Jesus quoted the scriptures every time Satan tried to tempt Him, and Satan departed (Luke 4:1-14). To both Eve and Jesus, Satan acknowledged God's Word, but he tried to cause doubt, tried to twist the meaning, and tried to invoke human imagination to trump God's definitive words. Because we now know Satan's tactics, we are able to use God's Word to discern truth and defeat the enemy!

In the transcribed translation of the 'Tao Te Ching', and the Biblical comparison, the entire Gospel of Christ Jesus is presented. The serpent is the yang to God's yin. The 'Tao Te Ching' represents the **desires** of the serpent, and the comparative Bible verses give you the words to defeat him.

Perhaps you're wondering why you've never seen a literal translation before? Well, that's because Taoist interpreters don't seek Truth, they suppress it with their own imaginations by adding and/or changing the words in the Word Range Translation or in their interpretations. Romans 1:18 says, "The wrath of God is being revealed from heaven against all the godlessness and wickedness of people, <u>who suppress the truth</u> by their wickedness".

Some interpreters say that they change words from the Word Range in an effort to "westernize" the Tao, while others say that interpretation is "in the eye of the beholder". To "westernize" means the Eastern philosophy must change to become palatable for the

American/European philosopher, while to "interpret" means the philosophy itself must change to become palatable for the individual. Both denote a deliberate effort to lose authenticity -- but what authenticity? of the author? the content?

That answer becomes clear when you read the literal (true) translation. The 'Tao Te Ching' consists of Satan's agenda to promote an amoral ideology for those who want to reject Truth -- for those who want to reject CHRIST. The pictography contains hints, notions, and nuances, all meant to encourage the "expert" Chinese translator/interpreter along.

To create an interpretation, the interpreter relies on their own thoughts, never selecting the true words of the dragon, Li Er, or if they do, always changing them to make them more palatable. Once the interpreter fills in the blanks with their desired reality, the goal is accomplished. They have rejected Truth and replaced Him with their own imagination. They have bitten the apple in order to eat from the "Tree of Knowledge of Good and Evil" (Genesis 2:17).

The truest state of any philosophy is its original intention. Taoists' have not realized who authored the 'Tao Te Ching' before now, because they have ignored the evidence of a pre-existing spiritual reality, one that cannot be changed through the filters of their own interpretation or imagination. All philosophy originates from one history, and that one history contains the evidence of ONE Truth. For example, did Taoism come up with the dark serpent named Liar, who tempts man into not believing God's Word? No. You have to go all the way back to the Garden of Eden to find the original thought (sin) and the serpent who said, "hath God said?". The 'Tao Te Ching' **proves** the accuracy and the reliability of the Biblical description of spiritual warfare. Do you really not see the irony of Taoism? I hope that you gain understanding of the spiritual battle that you are in -- before it's too late. Those of us who are following Bible prophecy realize that the Lord's return will be very soon. I don't know how much you know about "End Time" prophecy, but Jesus provided signs to know when His Kingdom was near (Luke 21:31; Matthew 24:6).

THE LETTER TO MY MOTHER-IN-LAW

His Word tells us that "the end" is actually an arrival of "the Kingdom of God" and that many things will transpire first. His Word explains the coming events in detail so that we will know what to expect and so that we will not be afraid. Then, His Word provides us with signs to look for leading up to those events, so that we can be guarded and mindful of the significance pertaining to everything going on around us. If we want to know where we are in prophecy, we can look at Israel. Israel is God's prophetic time clock. In 1948, Israel was reinstated and restored in their land after almost 2,000 years of banishment. This fulfilled many prophecies! And the Lord said that the generation that sees Israel bloom again, would be the generation to see the Lord's coming (Matthew 24:34).

There are many, many, other prophecies that support the realization that we are THAT generation. In fact, those who study prophecy point to the "convergence" of so many fulfilled prophecies, as the "sign of all signs", or the biggest sign of all!

Each of us has a spot in prophecy whether we believe God's Word or not, so choose ye this day whom you will serve -- God The Father or the Father of Lies (Joshua 24:15).

In order to aid in your understanding of the comparison, I've underlined the ideas, concepts, or words, that are being compared or contrasted, and mirrored them opposite each other on the pages. I have made some sentences and/or words **bold**, because I want you to realize a connection between them -and they were located far apart on the mirrored pages. I used several different Bible translations in the comparison, but I always cross-reference with The King James Version to ensure accuracy. Perhaps, it should be noted that Bible translations vary in their footnotes and in their terminology --but should not vary the meaning of the original text.

I will continue to pray that you will decide to trust the Lord!

With much love,

A Word From Me (The Daughter-in-law)

A WORD FROM ME (THE DAUGHTER-IN-LAW)

I want to take a moment to thank anyone who might be reading the "book" that I've worked so hard on. I use the word book sparingly because I contributed only a small portion of my own writing, and the rest is the quoted words of God the Father, next to the words of the 'Tao Te Ching'. I hope you will find this comparison to be thought-provoking and enjoyable, but more importantly, to be a convincing evidence for the truth of the Bible. My prayer is that every last one of my friends and family would come to have a personal relationship with Jesus.

The discussion of opposing religions can be controversial, however, I want to assure you that my mother-in-law and I remain on good terms. No relationships were harmed in the making of this book! I hope that you will also have a positive experience reading this, but I am aware of the fact that Christians are criticized when others feel convicted. God's Word convicts us all, but please know that this book was written out of love and concern for my mother-in-law's eternal well-being, and only secondarily published for anyone else who might be searching for a Biblical perspective on the 'Tao Te Ching' and Taoism. I have nothing but admiration for the woman who brought into this world, the most amazing, handsome, and honorable man that I've ever met. From the value system that she instilled in her son, he has chosen to make the Lord Jesus the King of his life. My sweet husband is a man of God, and his relationship with the Lord has benefited me greatly.

Perhaps you may feel that by my challenging my mother-in-laws beliefs, I'm being disrespectful. I can assure you that my speaking up is not because I don't appreciate her, but rather, specifically because I do! I hope and pray that my mother-in-law will choose to trust the Lord, so that she will be with the rest of her believing family for eternity. As a Christian, even if I thought my mother-in-law would hate me, I would still present her with the Biblical perspective on Taoism.

A WORD FROM ME (THE DAUGHTER-IN-LAW)

This is because I would rather be hated by her, than live with the idea that I didn't try to help her assimilate this life in the light of truth. In addition to not benefiting from a relationship with the Lord now, I also know that her choice will cause her to be permanently separated from God for all of eternity. Honestly, I believe that my not speaking the truth to her would be a hateful response to having learned of her belief in Taoism.

Perhaps you're wondering why I would write a book instead of just having an in-depth conversation with her? My answer to that is simple. I am not an eloquent speaker and this book is able to present the difficult subject of spiritual warfare far more effectively than any conversation with me ever could. This book is a "show and tell", with as much evidence as I could gather, and with translations/illustrations. Whereas, a conversation would be an attempted tell, with zero show.

Now, you're probably thinking that I could have written this book without addressing it specifically to my mother-in-law, right? To that I would say, yes, I could have. However, I see two problems with that idea. One, it avoids the truth as though real life circumstances and spiritual battles are to be covered up or made to appear as something other than what they are. The suggestion being that I could write a book about the pitfalls of deception from a place of deception, or write about reality, as I personally avoid or sugarcoat it.

The second reason is this, I'm writing this book not as a Bible scholar who has a doctorate in theology, but rather, I'm writing as an every day believer who is facing the same battles that we all face. We don't need doctorates to battle the enemy, we only need God's Word. Only God can reveal Himself to you, or me, and a doctorate wouldn't help without a relationship with Christ. His Word tells us that the Holy Spirit will help us with what to pray, will bring to memory the Lord's teaching, and that God is the Author and Finisher of our faith (Romans 8:26; John 14:26; Hebrews 12:2).

A WORD FROM ME (THE DAUGHTER-IN-LAW)

So, really, all we can say is, "Lord I believe, help my unbelief, reveal yourself to me, I want to know you, make your home in my heart". Then, we study and pray, and He reveals. The Lord will groom us for His good pleasure and purpose. Through His teaching, and through our experiential trials, we are expected to realize that a big difference exists between us and Him, and then we are expected to seek His righteousness, and not our own. Jesus said, "have you not read...?" (Matthew 19:4). Meaning, He expects us to read His Word and use our own understanding, logic, and reasoning to make the necessary judgments in order to arrive in His future Kingdom. His Word teaches us to think, because He wants to be our choice, the same way we are His.

I believe the Lord has, in a way, groomed me to challenge deceptions like Taoism. From early on in my working life, my interests have always pitted me against 'deception', in one way or another. First, I was a paralegal, where I learned to do research and make the case against "unfair or deceptive" practices. That lead me to study for the law enforcement exam, because I wanted to make detective, which lead to my studying Private Investigating instead. (Long story there.) That education lead me to work in the field of theft detection and loss prevention. So, it seems that I've always had it out for cheaters, liars, and thieves. Of course, I have taken other, unrelated jobs, but I believe that my path has always been directed by God. After all, it was one of the other jobs that lead me to my amazing husband, which lead to my "debunking" the idea that the serpent, Li Er, is a myth. If it weren't so sad, it would be funny. That said, I don't think my job-training alone has prepared me for confronting spiritual deception wherever I see it, but rather, I believe that having the tenacity to fight for the truth is the real key. If we aren't persistent when it comes to truth, then the truth is wasted on us. We aren't worthy of it.

A WORD FROM ME (THE DAUGHTER-IN-LAW)

I believe that we should be willing to stand up for the truth at all cost, including family relationships, or even at the cost of our heads for that matter (Revelation 20:4). I believe the Apostle Paul was called by God because of his tenacity. What if, after learning the truth, Paul decided to go home and live out a quiet, peaceful life? What if he feared what others would say or do when he spoke the truth? When Jesus revealed Himself to Paul, Paul was already diligently fighting for the preservation of God's Word. The Lord knew that Paul would continue on with the same zeal, but now with the correct message of Jesus. Thus, thanks to Paul and many others like him, you and I have the Gospel message.

I realize that confronting the unbelief of one's mother-in-law may seem taboo, but Jesus is the controversial One. I'm just a person who believes and loves everything He has to say. Jesus said that He would be the dividing line for us in this present age. There will be peace for believers in the future, but unfortunately, that would be after the unbelieving and rebellious are eliminated by God Himself. My goal, and the goal of all true believers, is to make disciples out of everyone we meet so that no one we know will fall into the category of 'unbelieving and rebellious'. Jesus said, "Do you think I came to bring peace on earth? No, I tell you, but division. From now on there will be five in one family divided against each other, three against two and two against three. They will be divided, father against son and son against father, mother against daughter and daughter against mother, mother-in-law against daughter-in-law and daughter-in-law against mother-in-law" (Luke 12:51-53). Jesus didn't sugarcoat this for us and His prophecy is made true by those who abandon the truth, not by those who speak it.

There will be a day when the Lord separates the sheep from the goats, but until then, I hope to have many more opportunities to speak with family members about God's Plan.

A WORD FROM ME (THE DAUGHTER-IN-LAW)

Since I seem determined to persuade everyone to the truth of the Bible, perhaps I should take a minute to explain why I am a Christian. I'm a Christian because Christianity is the only Faith in existence that expresses the attributes of a loving, merciful, and caring Person, Who is our Creator, and Who is as knowable and as relatable as you, or I. We need only look in the proverbial mirror to see if what the Bible says about us is true. We are made in His image, with all the same emotions and attributes that He has. Thus, not only can we have a relationship with the "deity" found in Christianity (The Lord Jesus), but that relationship is a mutually beneficial one. His love benefits us (Life/Blessings) and our love benefits Him (His Church/Bride). But by the same token, we are capable of hurting and offending the Lord. We can offend Him by way of ignoring Him, rejecting Him, or blaspheming His name, or even our lack of love toward one another, etc. These things affect Him personally. Christianity is the only Faith in the world in which our mortal situational ethics are exclusively pertaining to love, and have definite and knowable, immortal, and eternal consequences.

Everything we believe, do, and say, has eternal reward or eternal loss of reward. And that's only IF we're believers. For unbelievers, it's an eternity without Christ (hell). This fact means that we should first be responsive in our relationship with the Lord; and second, be faithful to love others with His love, not our own. We are to speak the sometimes unappreciated truth to others, out of love, regardless of the human consequences that might be imposed on us. Before He ascended, Jesus charged us to, "love each other **as** I have loved you". His Love never took the politically or socially correct approach with anyone, because He knew it would harm them in the long run. (In the eternal realm.) He was never sensitive to the delicate human ego or pride. The things that He said, once they were understood in context of the big picture, always seem to raise the bar of human intellect and understanding in the spiritual realm. He always spoke the truth boldly at the risk of His own human life, and He told all of His followers to do the same. I'm paraphrasing here, but He said, 'if you're following me you will be persecuted and hated the same way that they hated Me'. The 'they' being those who resented and killed Him (Mark 13:13; John 15:18). Jesus made it clear that if you love your life more than Him, you will lose it; and if you lose your life for His sake, you will find it (Luke 9:24). He said if you love your family more than Him, you're not worthy of Him (Matthew 10:37).

It was only after God had explained everything to us in writing through His prophets, apostles, scribes, and messengers; and only after He had modeled human history so as to explain everything using types and shadows (wow!); and only after demonstrating His Power and Authority throughout the generations through prophecy and miracles; and only after using symbolism throughout His explanations (wow!); and only after placing signs in the sky; and only after He personally explained all things to us in sermons and in parables, while at the same time demonstrating everything in His own human living; and it was only after He became the Sacrificial Lamb and was raised from the dead three days later; and it was only after He sent the Holy Spirit to guide you and me; and it was only after He had explained everything in so many different ways that the convergence of such into one cohesive book (the Bible), could be nothing less than a miracle! -- it is only NOW, that the ball is now in our court.

We can look at all of creation and know that there is a God. Then we can read God's Autobiography -The Bible- to know Him personally! I am a Christian because there will never be a deity with more proof of power and authority, who uses it in a more loving way. Now, the burden of proof is on those of us who DO believe God's Word.

A WORD FROM ME (THE DAUGHTER-IN-LAW)

What we believe, say we believe, and do about what we say we believe, should all match up. If any of these don't align, we should repent to the Lord and change according to His Life in us. This is the process of growing in Him. We allow Him to teach and lead us into a consistent testimony for His Name's Sake. This is not a testimony for others to see, but a testimony for our own salvation. If we want to enter His Kingdom, we have to measure ourselves with His standard of righteousness, and not man's standard. The confession of our mouth validates our intention, while our actions either validate, or contradict both. We can't bluff God, because He knows exactly who we're living our lives for (ourselves or Him). However, we can and will bluff ourselves. God's Word is the Light that helps us all see our own inner condition, apart from man's ideals and concepts of righteousness. Our salvation is no small feat.

God teaches us His reasoning in order that we might see how flawed our own is, and with that revelation, determine to learn His Ways. This makes Christianity a "God-centered" belief system, and not a "man-centered" belief system, which sets it apart from all other humanistic beliefs. This is evidence of God's "logic" and not man's. The Truth of God's Word is known by the appearance of God's logic in His Word. For example, if Christianity were developed by man, and not God, why would man condemn his own private thoughts (lust/covet/envy)? Only God could know man's thoughts. And why would man say to love your enemy? Likewise, this also makes man's logic the key to identifying the untruth found in all other religions. For example, the logic of Islam: wage jihad and murder all non-muslims in the name of Allah and win a free pass into paradise, where you'll get to deflower seventy-two intelligent (but soulless), virgins. Would a moral authority entice wrongdoing, using another wrong doing as the reward? Then there's the logic of New Age: we're all gods. Well, if we're all god's, who set the standard?

A WORD FROM ME (THE DAUGHTER-IN-LAW)

Who created life from non-life? Then there are Buddhists: there is no God, but we can meditate into a nirvana and end the continuous cycle of life and death. If there's no supernatural, how are Buddhists in a continuous cycle of life? Lastly, there's Taoism: you can believe the words of the dragon, Li Er, but words have no meaning. If these beliefs did not have very sad, deadly, and devastating eternal consequences, they would be hysterically funny.

Only Christians believe in a God who is loving and approachable; who teaches us how to rise above our fallen human nature and to think logically so as to not be deceived by Satan. Jesus teaches us to watch out for our own human nature, false teachings, the traditions of men, and for false prophets. He says that we will know them by their fruit, which means that the God of the Bible is telling us to use our brains! Only a God willing to risk it all for true love tells you everything you need to know -- the good, the bad, and the ugly -- and then lets you use your own observation skills, logic, and reasoning to determine if He is telling you the truth or not.

I'm sorry if this news is disappointing to those who don't want to submit to an authority figure, but the good news is, He's a very cool God! He wants to share His Kingdom with us. It amazes me that other "religions" are as popular as they are. I believe the reason they're so popular isn't because of what they teach, but rather, because of what they don't teach. They don't teach eternal damnation (the ugly). Instead, you get chance after chance in life after life. There is no punishment, only the possible lack of reward in this life. There is no sin, only bad behavior which will come back to you as karma. They don't teach that you will stand before God to be judged.

I believe that this life is a series of tests placed upon each one of us to determine our intentions and mature us accordingly. The choices we make can only stem from one of two belief systems: our own, or God's. God's Word is the lamp to our feet and the light for our path (Psalm 119:105).

Jesus said that if we are to be saved, we must confess with our mouth that "Jesus is Lord", and believe in our heart that God raised Him from the dead (Romans 10:9). And then He said, "faith without works is dead" (James 2:17). Meaning that if we say we believe God's Word, but don't live according to it, then our confession is null and void. If we believe Jesus, Who said that "belief in Him" is the only way to enter into His Kingdom (John 14:6), but we choose not to speak to others about Him, do we really believe what Jesus said? Or, is it just that we don't really care where others will spend their eternity, so long as we're "saved"? The latter would mean we don't understand Jesus' teaching on love. His standard for love is much higher than man's standard. How are we going to love our enemies if we don't care where our own family spends eternity?

If a believer in Christ Jesus says, "Each person has their own path to God", then that person is an apostate. They are advocating a teaching or belief that is opposed to God's Word. There is but one way to the Father and that is through His Son, Jesus (John 14:6).

I could go on and on, but in closing, I pray that this book will help others to identify the truth by recognizing deception, and thus, better understand how spiritual battles are won or lost. I hope that this book will inspire those who DO believe to stand firm in God's Word and fight the good fight. Again, thanks for reading this. I hope to see you in His Kingdom!

If you have any thoughts you would like to share with me, you can contact me at:
AnonymousDaughterInLaw@Hushmail.com

~The Anonymous Daughter-in-law

The Response From My Mother-in-law

The Response From My Mother-in-law

Dear Daughter-in-law,

I appreciate all the work and effort you have put forth in order to understand the Tao de Ching. I also very much appreciate your concern for my spiritual health and salvation.

My first disclaimer however is that I am not a Taoist. I found the Tao de Ching to contain many truths. It was interesting to me in my exploration of Eastern thought. I found Shinto interesting to pursue when I was studying Japan. Were I to go to India, I would pursue Hinduism and the ancient Vedic literature. I believe that these and many other religions provide and provided a path to God. Many of them existed before the birth of Jesus or the compilation of the Bible.

My understanding of God has necessarily evolved from my own experience and from my roots in Christianity. Many ideas have accordingly come from my education in the Old and New Testament. Religious labels in general are not meaningful to me. I believe Jesus was fully human with a God infused presence that filled him with the wisdom and power that is transferred to all believers.

I believe that the Bible is a God inspired group of historical books written by ancient authors in ancient times. I do not believe that God dictated the Bible word for word any more that He dictated the Koran or the Tao or the Vedic literature or any other of the sacred texts. God to me is a real presence. God in Jesus Christ is a real presence. I look at my life as a journey into the mystery of God.

Maybe life itself is this journey with this Presence.

The Response From My Mother-in-law

Most of the sacred texts purport an afterlife and devil like characters who influence humans to sin.

I do not believe in Satan though it is obvious that sin and evil exist. I do not believe in an after life per se although this is unknowable.

You and I have discussed how words can be interpreted and meaning gleaned all according to the reader's perspective. Depending on how one uses the "clay of the Tao to fashion a pot of thought" The Tao could be interpreted as coming from Lucifer or as coming from God.

Thank you for your caring.

Peace and love,
Mother-in law

The Tao Te Ching of Lao Tzu
(The Way Power Book of Old Master)
By: The Old Master/Ancient Serpent/Father of Lies
Transcribed Translation By:
The Anonymous Daughter-in-law

Next To...

God's Word, The Holy Bible
By: Our Heavenly Father
(Through Forty Of His Prophets)

The Tao Te Ching - Chapter 1

Way can <u>speak</u>, wrong constant Way.
道可道,非常道。
<u>Name can name</u>, wrong constant name.
名可名,非常名。

Without name heaven earth, it <u>begin</u>.
无名天地,之始。

Have name, <u>ten thousand things</u> it mother.
有名,万物之母。

Reason constant <u>without desire,</u> so as to observe its clever.
故常无欲,以觀其妙。
<u>Constant have desire</u>, so as to observe its border.
常有欲,以觀其徼。

<u>This two person</u> same <u>out come</u>, but different name.
此兩者同出,而异名。
Together call it dark.
同謂之玄。

Dark it also <u>mysterious</u>, crowd wonderful it <u>gate</u>.
玄之又玄,众妙之门。

The Holy Bible

And <u>God said</u>, "Let there be light," and there was light.
Genesis 1:3
For "everyone who calls on <u>the name of the Lord</u> will be saved."
Romans 10:13

In the <u>beginning</u> was the Word, and the Word was with God, and the Word was God. John 1:1
I am Alpha and Omega, the beginning and the ending, saith the Lord, which is, and which was, and which is to come, the Almighty.
Revelation 1:8

<u>All things</u> were made through him, and without him was not any thing made that was made. John 1:3

Yet they say to God, 'Leave us alone! We have <u>no desire</u> to know your ways. Job 21:14
<u>Blessed are they which do hunger and thirst after righteousness</u>: for they shall be filled. Submit yourselves therefore to God.
Matthew 5:6

The Word was the source of life, and this life brought light to mankind. The <u>light</u> shines in the <u>darkness</u>. John 1:4-5
To open their eyes, and **to turn them from darkness to light, and from the power of Satan unto God**, that they may receive forgiveness of sins, and inheritance among them which are sanctified by faith that is in me. Acts 26:18

And without controversy, great is the <u>mystery</u> of godliness:
1 Timothy 3:16
Then said Jesus unto them again, Verily, verily, I say unto you, I am the <u>door</u> of the sheep. John 10:7
And I say also unto thee, That thou art Peter, and upon this rock I will build my church; and the <u>gates of hell</u> shall not prevail against it. Matthew 16:18

The Tao Te Ching - Chapter 2

Under heaven, everybody know <u>beauty</u>, it serve as beauty.
天下，皆知美，之為美。
This evil stop.
斯惡已。

Everybody know <u>good, serve as good</u>.
皆知善，之為善。
This not good, stop. 斯不善，已。

<u>Death have no appearance life</u>, difficult change appearance <u>finished</u>. 故有无相生，難易相成。
Forever lack appearance, look high low, appearance to overturn. 长短相，形高下，相傾。

Sound voice appearance peaceful before <u>future</u> appearance follow. 音声相和前后相随。

Correct according sage man, dwell not have <u>do his work</u>, do not say his teaching.
是以圣人，处无無之事，行不言之教。

Ten thousand things arise, yet no <u>speech</u>.
万物作焉，而不辞。
Grow and yet, not exist. 生而，不有。
Do, yet <u>not rely on</u>, achievement finish, yet not live.
行，而不恃，功成，而弗居。

Man only not live, so as to <u>not leave</u>.
夫唯弗居，是以不去。

The Holy Bible

He hath made every thing <u>beautiful</u> in his time.
Ecclesiastes 3:11
For the invisible things of him from the creation of the world are clearly seen, <u>being understood by the things that are made</u>, even his eternal power and Godhead; so that they are without excuse:
Romans 1:20

A <u>good man bringeth forth good things</u>: and an evil man bringeth forth evil things.
Matthew 12:35

Truly, truly, I say to you, whoever hears my word and believes Him who sent me has eternal life. He does not come into judgment, but has passed <u>from death to life</u>.
John 5:24

When he had received the drink, Jesus said, "It is <u>finished</u>." With that, he bowed his head and gave up his spirit.
John 19:30

In the <u>future</u> there is laid up for me the crown of righteousness, which the Lord, the righteous Judge, will award to me on that day; and not only to me, but also to all who have loved His <u>appearing</u>.
2 Timothy 4:8

<u>Do all things</u> in the name of the Lord Jesus.
Colossians 3:17

He who heareth these <u>sayings of mine</u>, and doeth them, I will liken him unto a wise man.
Matthew 7:24

My salvation and my honor <u>depend on God</u>; he is my mighty rock, my refuge.
Psalm 62:7

<u>Now this is eternal life</u>: that they know the only true God.
John 17:3

The Tao Te Ching - Chapter 3

No value virtuous, cause people not argue.
不尚賢，使民不爭。

Not expensive to obtain it commodity, enable people not act as thief. 不貴得之貨，使民不為盜。

No see able to desire, cause people mind not in confusion.
不见可欲，使民心不乱。

Right according to sage man of order, empty their mind, seed their belly, weak their will, strong their bone.
是以圣人之治，虛其心，实其腹，弱其志，强其骨。

Often use people without knowing, without desire, to employ man wisdom. 常使民无知，无欲，使夫智。
Person not dare act, too. 者不敢為，也。

Do without do, follow multitude, not rules.
為无為，則無，不治。

The Holy Bible

<u>Let another man praise thee</u>, a stranger, and not thine own lips.
Proverbs 27:2

What we have received is not the spirit of the world, but the Spirit who is from God, so that we may understand what God has <u>freely given us</u>. 1 Corinthians 2:12

This righteousness is given through faith in Jesus Christ to all who believe. There is no difference between Jew and Gentile, for all have sinned and fall short of the glory of God, and all are justified freely by his grace through the redemption that came by Christ Jesus. Romans 3:22-24

<u>See, I have set before thee this day life and good</u>, and death and evil; Deuteronomy 30:15

<u>Who is wise</u> and understanding among you? Let them show it by their good life, by deeds done, in the humility that comes from wisdom. James 3:13

Be alert and of sober mind. <u>Your enemy the devil prowls around like a roaring lion looking for someone to devour.</u> 1 Peter 5:8

Let no man deceive himself. If any man among you <u>seemeth to be wise</u> in this world, let him become a fool, that he may be wise. For the wisdom of this world is foolishness with God. For it is written, "He taketh the wise in their own craftiness".
1 Corinthians 3:18-19

<u>See to it that no one takes you captive</u> through philosophy and empty deception, according to the tradition of men, according to the elementary principles of the world, <u>rather than according to Christ</u>. Colossians 2:8

The Tao Te Ching - Chapter 4

The <u>Way infuse and employ his confusion</u> to not be filled.
道冲而用之或不盈。

<u>Abyss</u>! Similar to ten thousand creatures his ancestry.
渊兮！似万物之宗。

Oppress their sharp. Divide their disorderly. <u>Mix their light with his dirt</u>. 挫其銳。 解其紛。和其光同其尘。

Clear! Appearing <u>possibly</u> survived. 湛兮！似或存。

<u>We not know Whose Son</u>, appearance the <u>Supreme Being of First</u>. 吾不知誰之子，象帝之先。

The Holy Bible

For <u>God is not the author of confusion</u>, but of peace, as in all churches of the saints.   1 Corinthians 14:33

Jesus asked him, "What is your name?" "Legion," he replied, because many demons had gone into him. And they begged Jesus repeatedly not to order them to go into the <u>Abyss</u>.
Luke 8:30-31

Again Jesus spoke to them, saying, "I am the light of the world. <u>Whoever follows me will not walk in darkness, but will have the light of life</u>."   John 8:12

You adulterous people, don't you know that friendship with the world means enmity against God? Therefore, anyone who chooses to be a friend of the world becomes an enemy of God.
James 4:4

Then he said to Thomas, "Put your finger here, and see my hands; and put out your hand, and place it in my side. <u>Do not disbelieve, but believe</u>."   John 20:27

Who is the liar? It is <u>whoever denies that Jesus is the Christ.</u> Such a person is the antichrist--denying <u>the Father</u> and the Son.
1 John 2:22

The Tao Te Ching - Chapter 5

<u>Heaven earth</u> not humane, use all things on earth act as hay dogs. 天地不仁，以万物為芻狗。

Wikipedia: Straw dogs were used as ceremonial objects in ancient China. Su Zhe's commentary on this verse explains: "Heaven and Earth are not partial. They do not kill living things out of cruelty or give them birth out of kindness. We do the same when we make straw dogs to use in sacrifices. We dress them up and put them on the altar, but not because we love them. And when the ceremony is over, we throw them into the street, but not because we hate them."

Sage man not humane, <u>use common people serve as hay dogs</u>. 圣人不仁，以百姓為芻狗。

Heaven earth these separate, this despite opening at both ends key? 天地之间，其犹橐籥乎？

<u>Emptiness yet not bend, stir but recover to go beyond</u>. 虚而不屈，动而愈出。

Many word count exhaust, <u>not in accordance with guard center</u>. 多言数穷，不如守中。

The Holy Bible

<u>Heaven and earth</u> shall pass away, but my words shall not pass away.   Matthew 24:35

<u>Do to others as you would have them do to you</u>. "If you love those who love you, what credit is that to you? Even sinners love those who love them.   Luke 6:31-32

But love your enemies, do good to them, and lend to them without expecting to get anything back. Then your reward will be great, and you will be children of the Most High, because he is kind to the ungrateful and wicked.   Luke 6:35

So then, as we have opportunity, let us do good to everyone, and especially to those who are of the household of faith.
                               Galatians 6:10

Therefore, each of us will give an account of himself to God.
                               Romans 14:12

Let no one deceive you with <u>empty words</u>.   Ephesians 5:6

Beloved, believe not every spirit, but try the spirits whether they are of God: because many false prophets are gone out into the world.   1 John 4:1

<u>Discretion will guard you</u>, understanding will watch over you.
                               Proverbs 2:11

The Tao Te Ching - Chapter 6

Gorge God <u>not to death</u>, believe name profound female.
谷神不死，是謂玄牝。

Profound female his door to be called <u>God ground foundation</u>.
玄牝之門是謂天地根。

Soft cotton similar to life, use this to <u>not be diligent</u>.
綿綿若存，用之不勤。

The Holy Bible

Jesus said unto her, <u>I am the resurrection</u>, and the life: he that believeth in me, though he were dead, yet shall he live:
John 11:25

Who alone has **immortality**, dwelling in unapproachable light, whom no man has seen nor can see, to whom be honor and eternal might. Amen.
1 Timothy 6:16

For as the woman originates from the man, so also the man has his birth through the woman; and <u>all things originate from God</u>.
1 Corinthians 11:12

Therefore, brethren, <u>be all the more diligent</u> to make certain about His calling and choosing you; for as long as you practice these things, you will never stumble; for in this way the entrance into the eternal kingdom of our Lord and Savior Jesus Christ will be abundantly supplied to you.
2 Peter 1:10-11

The Tao Te Ching - Chapter 7

God eternal, <u>earth time passing</u>. 天长,地久。
Heaven earth location, reason able forever, not only long time person. 天地所,以能长,且久者。

Thus, his not have beginning birth, cause able <u>forever life</u>.
以,其不自生,故能长生。

This reason sage man behind his body, yet life first. <u>Out side his body yet, life survive</u>.
是以圣人后其身,而身先。外其身而,身存。

Oppose commands that not have secret! Thus, <u>energy become their secret</u>. 非以其无私邪! 故,能成其私。

The Holy Bible

In the <u>beginning</u> God created the heavens and the earth.
Genesis 1:1

I am the Alpha and the Omega, the First and the Last, **the Beginning and the End.** Revelation 22:13

For the one who sows to his own flesh will from the flesh reap corruption, but the one who sows to the Spirit will from the Spirit reap <u>eternal life</u>. Galatians 6:8

Whoever believes in the Son has **eternal life**, but whoever rejects the Son will not see life, for God's wrath remains on them.
John 3:36

We are confident, I say, and willing rather to be <u>absent from the body, and to be present with the Lord</u>. 2 Corinthians 5:8

For this purpose also I labor, striving according to <u>His power, which mightily works within me</u>. Colossians 1:29

But the magicians did the same things by **their secret arts**; they also made frogs come up on the land of Egypt.
Exodus 8:7

And no wonder, for **Satan himself masquerades as an angel of light.** 2 Corinthians 11:14

The Tao Te Ching - Chapter 8

<u>Highest good like water</u>. 上善若水。

<u>Water good benefit</u> ten thousand things, yet not contend.
水善利万物，而不争。

<u>Deal with many men him actually hate</u>, <u>cause some according to the Way</u>. 處众人之所惡，故几于道。

Dwell good person land. Soul <u>good person</u> deep. Engage good person kindness. Speak good person message.
居善地。 心善渊。 与善仁。 言善信。

Government good person <u>execute</u>. 正善治。

Work good person energy to use good person opportune moment.
事善能动善时。

Man alone not <u>contend</u>, reason not outstanding.
夫唯不争，故无尤。

The Holy Bible

The <u>water I give them, will become in them eternal life</u>.
John 4:14

"He who believes in Me, as the Scripture said, 'From his innermost being will flow <u>rivers of living water</u>.'"   John 7:38

"You have heard that it was said, 'You shall love your neighbor and hate your enemy.' But I say to you, <u>Love your enemies and pray for those who **persecute you**</u>, that you may be children of your Father in heaven. He causes his sun to rise on the evil and the good, and sends rain on the righteous and the unrighteous.
Matthew 5:43-45

For to this you have been called, because **Christ also suffered** for you, leaving you an example, <u>so that you might follow in His steps</u>.
1 Peter 2:21

And Jesus said to him, "Why do you call Me good? <u>No one is good</u> **except God alone**.   Mark 10:18

They will put you out of the synagogues. Indeed, the hour is coming when **whoever kills you will think he is offering service to God**.
John 16:2

Thou shalt not kill.   Exodus 20:13

<u>Fight the good fight</u> of the faith. Take hold of the eternal life to which you were called when you made your good confession in the presence of many witnesses.   1 Timothy 6:12

The Tao Te Ching - Chapter 9

Grasp and <u>fill</u> not in accordance with his finish.
持而盈之不如其己。

Surmise and sharp, he not able always <u>protect</u>.
揣而銳,之不可長保。

Gold precious stones fill hall, is not <u>him competent protect</u>.
金玉滿堂,莫之能守。

<u>Rich</u>, expensive, and arrogant, naturally cause their mistake.
富,貴,而驕,自遺其咎。

Result go well, person to <u>decline God</u> him the Way.
功遂身退,天之道。

The Holy Bible

Do you not know that you are God's temple and that <u>God's Spirit dwells in you</u>?   1 Corinthians 3:16

Nevertheless, I tell you the truth: it is to your advantage that I go away, for if I do not go away, the Helper will not come to you. But if I go, I will send him to you.   John 16:7

Submit yourselves therefore to God. <u>Resist the devil</u>, and he will flee from you.   James 4:7

In You, O LORD, I have taken refuge; Let me never be ashamed. In Your righteousness deliver me and rescue me; Incline Your ear to me and save me. Be to me a rock of habitation to which I may continually come; You have given commandment to save me, For You are my rock and my fortress. <u>Rescue me</u>, O my God, out of the hand of the wicked, Out of the grasp of the wrongdoer and ruthless man.   Psalm 71:1-4

<u>Riches do not profit in the day of wrath</u>, but righteousness delivers from death.   Proverbs 11:4

Then said Jesus unto his disciples, Verily I say unto you, That a rich man shall hardly enter into the kingdom of heaven And again I say unto you, It is easier for a camel to go through the eye of a needle, than for a rich man to enter into the kingdom of God.   Matthew 19:23-24

Therefore, <u>anyone who rejects this instruction</u> does not reject a human being but God, the very God who gives you his Holy Spirit.   1 Thessalonians 4:8

The Tao Te Ching - Chapter 10

Load camp, <u>soul to hold</u>, one ability not leave?
載營,魄抱,一能無離乎?

Special spirit <u>to send gentle energy, such as infant son</u>?
專气致柔能,如嬰兒乎?

Wash away <u>mysterious view</u>, <u>energy not to have flaw</u>?
涤除玄覽,能无疵乎?

Love country, <u>rule the people</u>, energy not do?
愛國,治民,能无為乎?

God door open all, ability to serve as female?
天門開闔,能為雌乎?

Understand clear four, reach energy <u>not know</u>?
明白四,達能無知乎?

<u>Giving birth to Him</u>, <u>domestic animals him to grow</u>, but not to have; to serve yet, and not rely on; to develop yet, <u>not rule</u>; that called mysterious goodness.
生之,畜之生,而不有;為而,不恃;长而,不宰;是謂玄德。

The Holy Bible

"I, the LORD, have called you in righteousness; I will take hold of your hand. I will keep you and will make you to be a covenant for the people and a light for the Gentiles, to open eyes that are blind, <u>to free captives</u> from prison and to release from the dungeon those who sit in darkness.   Isaiah 42:6-7

For God so loved the world, <u>that he gave his only begotten Son</u>, that whosoever believeth in him should not perish, but have everlasting life. For God sent not his Son into the world to condemn the world; but that the world <u>through him might be saved</u>.   John 3:16-17

You know that He appeared in order to take away sins; **<u>and in Him there is no sin</u>**.   1 John 3:5

Not everyone who says to me, 'Lord, Lord,' will enter the kingdom of heaven, <u>but only the one who does the will of My Father</u> who is in heaven.   Matthew 7:21

This is good and acceptable in the sight of God our Savior, who desires <u>all men to be saved and to come to the knowledge of the truth</u>.   1 Timothy 2:3-4

Then God said, "<u>Let us make mankind</u> in our image, in our likeness, **<u>so that they may rule</u>** over the fish in the sea and the birds in the sky, over the livestock and all the wild animals, and over all the creatures that move along the ground."   Genesis 1:26

The Tao Te Ching - Chapter 11

<u>Three</u> complete roll, <u>together one wheel</u>.
三十幅,共一毂。

<u>To be such without,</u> exists vehicle him use.
当其无,有车之用。

<u>Mix water with clay soil, together make vessel</u>, of its nothing, have receptacle him use.
埏埴以為器,当其无,有器之用。

Chisel <u>door window to use for room</u>, when that not exist, **room him to use**.
鑿户牖以為室,当其无有,室之用。

Reason exist him to use for benefit, not him to use for use.
故有之以為利,无之以為用。

The Holy Bible

Go ye therefore, and teach all nations, baptizing them in the name of the <u>Father, and of the Son, and of the Holy Ghost</u>:
Matthew 28:19

One Lord, one faith, one baptism, <u>One God and Father of all</u>, who is above all, and through all, and in you all.   Ephesians 4:5-6

"<u>Whoever is not with me is against me</u>, and whoever does not gather with me scatters. "When an impure spirit comes out of a person, it goes through arid places seeking rest and does not find it. Then it says, 'I will return to the house I left.' When it arrives, it finds the house swept clean and put in order. Then it goes and takes seven other spirits more wicked than itself, and they go in and live there. And the final condition of that person is worse than the first."
Luke 11:23-26

<u>The LORD God formed a man from the dust of the ground</u> and breathed into his nostrils.
Genesis 2:7

When Jesus spoke again to the people, he said, "I am the light of the world. <u>Whoever follows me will never walk in darkness, but will have the light of life.</u>"
John 8:12

Therefore, if anyone cleanses himself from what is dishonorable, he will be a vessel for honorable use, set apart as holy, useful to the master of the house, ready for every good work.
2 Timothy 2:21

Do you not know that your bodies are temples of the Holy Spirit, who is in you, whom you have received from God? You are not your own;
1 Corinthians 6:19

The Tao Te Ching - Chapter 12

<u>Five</u> colors make man eye <u>blind</u>, 五色令人目盲，
<u>Five</u> sounds make man ear <u>deaf</u>, 五音令人耳，
<u>Five</u> tastes make man mouth frank, 五味令人口爽，

Quickly hasten cultivate hunt, cause man mind issue insane.
馳騁畋猎，令人心发狂。

Difficult obtain him goods cause man do harm.
難得之__令，人行妨。

This according to sage man, serve as <u>belly</u>, not serve as <u>eye</u>,
Reason, <u>remove that, take this</u>.
是以圣人為，腹不為目，故去彼取此。

The Holy Bible

How art thou fallen from heaven, O Lucifer, son of the morning! How art thou cut down to the ground, which didst weaken the nations!
For thou hast said in thine heart,

<u>1.</u> I will ascend into heaven,
<u>2.</u> I will exalt my throne above the stars of God:
<u>3.</u> I will sit also upon the mount of the congregation, in the sides of the north:
<u>4.</u> I will ascend above the heights of the clouds;
<u>5.</u> I will be like the most High.   Isaiah 12:12-14

The <u>blind</u> receive their sight, and the lame walk, the lepers are cleansed, and the <u>deaf</u> hear, the dead are raised up, and the poor have the gospel preached to them.   Matthew 11:5

Don't you see that whatever enters the mouth goes into the <u>stomach</u> and then out of the body? But the things that come out of a person's mouth come from the heart, and these defile them.
Matthew 15:17-18

If your right <u>eye</u> causes you to stumble, <u>gouge it out and throw it away</u>. It is better for you to lose one part of your body than for your whole body to be thrown into hell.
Matthew 5:29-30

The Tao Te Ching - Chapter 13

<u>Favor disgrace</u> like alarm. Valuable great suffering as oneself.
寵辱若惊。 貴大患若身。

Why say favor disgrace like <u>alarm</u>?
何謂寵辱若惊?

To favor considered as inferior. <u>Gain it like frightened, lose it like frightened</u>. 寵為下。 得之若惊，失之若惊。

That meaning favor disgrace like alarm.
是謂貴辱若惊。

Why say, valuable great suffering as oneself?
何謂，貴大患若身？

<u>I place together many suffering person</u>, become to be my body, and I not have body, <u>I have what suffering</u>?
吾所以有大患者，為吾有身，及吾无身，吾有何患？

Hence, valuable <u>relying upon body to serve as god below</u>.
故，貴以身為天下。
The same able to rely on god below, be fond of using the body god below.
若可寄天下，愛以身為天下。

You can hold in the palm, world. 若可託，天下。

The Holy Bible

He has shown His <u>favor</u> and taken away my disgrace.
Luke 1:25

For <u>by grace</u> you have been saved through faith; and that not of yourselves, it is the gift of God; not as a result of works, so that no one may boast.
Ephesians 2:8-9

So shalt thou find favor and good understanding in the sight of God and man.
Proverbs 3:4

Beware that your hearts are not deceived, and that you do not turn away and serve other gods and worship them.
Deuteronomy 11:16

When pride comes, then comes disgrace, but with humility comes wisdom.
Proverbs 11:2

<u>The LORD delights in those who fear Him</u>, who put their hope in His unfailing love.
Psalm 147:11

And <u>the devil who deceived them</u> was thrown into the lake of fire and brimstone, where the beast and the false prophet are also; and <u>they will be tormented day and night forever and ever</u>.
Revelation 20:10

But He gives a greater grace. Therefore it says, "GOD IS OPPOSED TO THE PROUD, BUT GIVES GRACE TO THE HUMBLE." Submit therefore to God. <u>Resist the devil and he will flee from you</u>.
James 4:6-7

The Tao Te Ching - Chapter 14

Look at him and <u>not see</u>, name called barbarian.
Listen him not hear name called hope.
Strike him not gain name called micro.
視之不見，名曰夷。 听之不聞名曰希。 搏之不得名曰微。

This <u>three</u> person not able to deliver restrain, reason confused and become one.
此三者不可致詰，故混而為一。

Their higher not bright, their lower not dark. <u>Restrain rope not able name</u>. Recover to go back in no matter.
其上不皦，其下不昧。 繩繩不可名。 复归于无無物。

That name not <u>appearance him</u> official, not substance him image. That name confused seemingly.
是謂无状之状，无物之象。 是謂惚恍。

Welcome him <u>not see him</u> first, follow him not see his back.
迎之不见其首，随之不见其后。

Grasp ancient him the Way, so as to defend modern him exist.
执古之道，以御今之有。
<u>Ability knowledge</u> ancient beginning is name the way discipline.
能知古始謂是道紀。

The Holy Bible

Though <u>you have not seen him</u>, you love him; and even though you do not see him now, you believe in him and are filled with an inexpressible and glorious joy, for you are receiving the end result of your faith, the salvation of your souls.
1 Peter 1:8-9

Therefore go and make disciples of all nations, baptizing them in the name of the <u>Father and of the Son and of the Holy Spirit</u>.
Matthew 28:19

For the secret power of lawlessness is already at work; but <u>the one who now holds it back will continue to do so till he is taken out of the way</u>. 2 Thessalonians 2:7

<u>The Word became flesh</u> and made his dwelling among us. We have seen his glory, the glory of the one and only Son, who came from the Father, full of grace and truth. 1 John 1:14

God said, "you <u>cannot see my face</u>, for no one may see me and live."
Exodus 33:20

Then Jesus told him, "Because you have seen me, you have believed; blessed are those who have not seen and yet have believed." John 20:29

These things I have written to you who believe in the name of the Son of God, <u>so that you may know</u> that you have eternal life.
1 John 5:13

The Tao Te Ching - Chapter 15

Ancient him be good at serve as <u>scholar person</u>, micro clever mysterious know well, profound not able to know.
古之善為士者，微妙玄通，深不可識。

Man only not able to know, <u>reason power to become him appearance.</u> 夫唯不可識，故強為之容。

Comfortable! Like winter to wade across river;
豫兮! 若冬涉川；

Scheme! To scare four neighbors; 猶兮! 若畏四鄰；

Majestic! <u>His identical appearance</u>; 儼兮! 其若容；

Scatter! Or ice these about to release; 渙兮! 若冰之將釋；

Honest! That as good as simple; 敦兮! 其若樸；

Wilderness! That as good as bewildered; 曠兮! 其若谷；

Mix! That as good as turbid; 混兮! 其若濁；

Tranquil! Such as if sea; 澹兮! 其若海；

Wind! As if without stop. 风兮! 若无止。

<u>Who able turbid and still him gentle clear</u>?
孰能濁以靜之徐清？

Who able calm and change him gentle life?
孰能安以动之徐生？

Maintain this Way, <u>not longing for full</u>. 保此道，者不欲盈。

Man only <u>not full</u>, reason able to shield and not <u>new become</u>.
夫唯不盈，故能蔽而新成。

The Holy Bible

<u>A wise man will hear and increase in learning</u>, And a man of understanding will acquire wise counsel, To understand a proverb and a figure. Proverbs 1:5-6

And no wonder, for even <u>Satan disguises himself as an angel of light</u>. 2 Corinthians 11:14

Let no one deceive you with empty words, for because of such things God's wrath comes on those who are disobedient. Ephesians 5:6

But if our gospel be hid, it is hid to them that are lost: In whom the god of this world (satan) hath blinded the minds of them which believe not, lest the light of the glorious gospel of Christ, <u>who is the image of God</u>, should shine unto them. 2 Corinthians 4:4

This is why I speak to them in parables: "Though seeing, they do not see; though hearing, they do not hear or understand. In them is fulfilled the prophecy of Isaiah: "'You will be ever hearing but never understanding; you will be ever seeing but never perceiving. Matthew 13:13-14

And he said unto them, Where is your faith? And they being afraid wondered, saying one to another, What manner of man is this! for <u>he commandeth even the winds and water, and they obey him</u>. Luke 8:25

Blessed are those who hunger and thirst for righteousness, for <u>they will be filled</u>. Matthew 5:6

Therefore <u>if any man be in Christ</u>, he is a new creature: old things are passed away; behold, <u>all things are become new</u>. 2 Corinthians 5:17

The Tao Te Ching - Chapter 16

<u>Present empty extreme</u>, protect motionless sincere.
致虛极，守静篤。

Myriad thing simultaneously make, I to use, behold <u>duplicate</u>.
万物并作，吾以，觀复。

Man creature ability to trick, each repeatedly <u>return to their foundation</u>. 夫物芸芸，各复归其根。

Return to root called motionless, that means, <u>repeat life</u>.
归根曰静，是謂，复命。

Repeat life called normal, recognize constant called brilliant.
复命曰常，知常曰明。

Not know constant, reckless serve as bad. 不知常，妄作凶。

Know always allow, 知常容，

allow only public, 容乃公，

public thus complete, 公乃全，

complete thus god, 全乃天，

god thus the Way, 天乃道，

the Way long <u>to end</u>, 道乃久，

no body not <u>dangerous</u>. 没身不殆。

The Holy Bible

He said to them, "Go into all the world and <u>preach the gospel</u> to all creation. Whoever believes and is baptized will be saved, but whoever does not believe will be condemned.   Mark 16:15-16

So Moses and Aaron went to Pharaoh and did just as the LORD commanded. Aaron cast down his staff before Pharaoh and his servants, and it became a serpent. Then Pharaoh summoned the wise men and the sorcerers, and they, the magicians of Egypt, <u>also did the same by their secret arts</u>. For each man cast down his staff, and they became serpents. But Aaron's staff swallowed up their staffs.   Exodus 7:10-12

<u>The heart is deceitful</u> above all things, and desperately wicked: who can know it?   Jeremiah 17:9

Jesus said to her, "I am the resurrection and the life; he who believes in Me will live even if he dies, and <u>everyone who lives and believes in Me will never die</u>.   John 11:25-26

When Jesus spoke again to the people, he said, "I am the light of the world. Whoever follows me will never walk in darkness, but will have the light of life."   John 8:12

"If I told you earthly things and you do not believe, how will you believe if I tell you heavenly things?"   John 3:12

As Jesus was sitting on the Mount of Olives, the disciples came to him privately. "Tell us," they said, "when will this happen, and what will be the sign of your coming and of the <u>end of the age</u>?"   Matthew 24:3

The prudent see <u>danger</u> and take refuge, but the simple keep going and pay the penalty.   Proverbs 22:3

The Tao Te Ching - Chapter 17

Very <u>superior</u>, <u>inferior</u> know exist him. 太上，下知有之。

His <u>order love and praise him</u>. 其次亲而譽之。

His order fear him. 其次畏之。

His order insult these. 其次侮之。

<u>Faith</u> <u>not enough here</u>, <u>have no trust</u> here.
信不足焉，有不信焉。

Long drawn out! <u>His noble speech</u>,
悠兮! 其貴言。

Achievement <u>accomplish incident favorable</u>, <u>numerous people all say</u>. 功成事遂，百姓皆謂。

I naturally like this. 我自然。

The Holy Bible

<u>Do not consider yourself to be superior</u> to those other branches. If you do, consider this: You do not support the root, but the root supports you. Romans 11:18

Blessed are the <u>meek</u>: for they shall inherit the earth. Matthew 5:5

Master, which is the great <u>commandment</u> in the law? Jesus said unto him, <u>Thou shalt love the Lord thy God with all thy heart, and with all thy soul, and with all thy mind</u>. This is the first and great commandment. And the second is like unto it, Thou shalt love thy neighbour as thyself. On these two commandments hang all the law and the prophets. Matthew 22:36-40

<u>And without faith it is impossible to please God</u>, because anyone who comes to Him must believe that He exists and that He rewards those who earnestly seek Him. Hebrews 11:16

For by grace **you have been saved through faith**; and that not of yourselves, it is the gift of God; Ephesians 2:8

<u>Trust in the LORD</u> with all your heart and lean not on your own understanding. Proverbs 3:5

He who trusts in himself is a fool, but he who walks in wisdom is kept safe. Proverbs 28:16

From that time on <u>Jesus began to preach</u>, "Repent, for the kingdom of heaven has come near." Matthew 4:17

And after the sixty-two weeks <u>Messiah will be cut off</u> and will have nothing; Daniel 9:26

"What shall I do, then, with the one you call the king of the Jews?" Pilate asked them. <u>"Crucify him!" they shouted</u>. "Why? What crime has he committed?" asked Pilate. But they shouted all the louder, "Crucify him!" Mark 15:12-14

The Tao Te Ching - Chapter 18

<u>The Great Way abolish</u>, <u>have humane justice</u>.
大道廢，有仁义。

<u>Intelligent wisdom, to go beyond have great fake</u>.
慧智，出有大偽。

Six relatives not peace, only <u>filial piety kind</u>; country reside darkness confusion, have devotion statesman.
六亲不和，有孝慈；国家昏乱，有忠臣。

The Holy Bible

<u>The LORD God **commanded** the man, saying</u>, "From any tree of the garden you may eat freely; but from the tree of the knowledge of good and evil you shall not eat, for in the day that you eat from it you will surely die." Genesis 2:16-17

Now we know that the law is good, if one uses it lawfully, understanding this, <u>that **the law is not laid down for the just but for the lawless and disobedient**</u>, for the ungodly and sinners, for the unholy and profane, for those who strike their fathers and mothers, for murderers, the sexually immoral, men who practice homosexuality, enslavers, liars, perjurers, and whatever else is contrary to sound doctrine, in accordance with the gospel of the glory of the blessed God with which I have been entrusted.
1 Timothy 1:8-11

<u>I will destroy the wisdom of the wise</u>, and I will thwart the cleverness of the intelligent. 1 Corinthians 1:19

"<u>Honor your father and mother</u>"--which is the first **commandment** with a promise-- so that it may go well with you and that you may enjoy long life on the earth." Ephesians 6:2-3

Anyone who loves their father or mother more than Me is not worthy of Me; anyone who loves their son or daughter more than Me is not worthy of Me. Matthew 10:37

Therefore, **as God's chosen people**, holy and dearly loved, clothe yourselves with compassion, kindness, humility, gentleness and patience. Colossians 3:12

The Tao Te Ching - Chapter 19

Sever holy, <u>discard knowledge</u>, people <u>benefit hundred fold</u>;
絕圣，弃智，民利百倍；

Sever kindness, abandon righteousness, <u>people resume filial pity kind</u>. 絕仁，弃义，民复孝慈。

<u>Sever skillful</u>, reject profit, robber traitor not exist.
絕巧，弃利，盗贼无有。

Then <u>three</u> by reason serve as culture, not satisfaction.
此三者以為文，不足。

Hence, make exist place to belong, catch sight of simple, embrace plain, <u>lose personal few desires</u>.
故，令有所属，见素，抱朴，少私寡欲。

The Holy Bible

The lips of the wise <u>spread knowledge</u>; not so the hearts of fools.
                                                                Proverbs 15:7

And everyone who has left houses or brothers or sisters or father or mother or wife or children or fields for My sake <u>will receive a hundred times</u> as much and will inherit eternal life.
                                                                Matthew 19:29

But he that received seed into the good ground is he that heareth the word, and understandeth it; which also beareth fruit, and bringeth forth, some an **hundredfold**, some sixty, some thirty.
                                                                Matthew 13:23

And the second is like it: '<u>Love your neighbor as yourself.</u>'
                                                                Matthew 22:39

But wishing to justify himself, he said to Jesus, "And who is my neighbor?"   Luke 10:29

But I say unto you, Love your enemies, bless them that curse you, do good to them that hate you, and pray for them which despitefully use you, and persecute you;   Matthew 5:44

So shall it be at the end of the world: the angels shall come forth, and <u>sever the wicked</u> from among the just, And shall cast them into the furnace of fire: there shall be wailing and gnashing of teeth.   Matthew 49:50

"Go therefore and make disciples of all the nations, baptizing them in the name of <u>the Father</u> and <u>the Son</u> and <u>the Holy Spirit</u>, teaching them to observe all that I commanded you; and lo, I am with you always, even to the end of the age." Matthew 28:19-20

Take delight in the LORD, and <u>He will give you the desires of your heart</u>.   Psalm 37:4

The Tao Te Ching - Chapter 20

<u>Sever learning have not grief</u>, participate in pander to each other. Remove to what extent?
絕学无忧，唯之与阿。 相去几何？

Good him <u>take part in hate</u>, appearance leave if expel?
善之与惡，相去若何？

Man his place fear, not able not fear.
人之所畏，不可不畏。

Uncultivated! Such not yet beg! 荒兮！其未央哉！

<u>Many people prosperous splendid</u>, go to enjoy great fast as joyful scale platform.
众人熙熙，如享太牢如春登台。

<u>I</u> alone be an anchor! 我独泊兮！
That not omen. Such as baby boy him not child.
其未兆。 如婴儿之未孩。
Lazy, lazy! yet not have place go back to.
儽，儽兮！若无所归。
Crowd people all have surplus, yet <u>I</u> alone seem lost.
众人皆有余，而我独若遗。
<u>I</u> foolish man of mind also! Confused, confused! Vulgar man, illustrious manifest. 我愚人之心也哉！沌，沌兮！俗人昭昭。
<u>I</u> alone dark faint; 我独昏昏；
Vulgar people observe inspect, <u>I</u> alone stuffy subdued.
俗人察察， 我独闷闷。
Crowd people all exist, yet <u>I</u> alone stupid and low.
众人皆有以，而我独顽且鄙。
<u>I</u> alone different to people, and value feeding the mother.
我独异于人，而貴食母。

The Holy Bible

All Scripture is breathed out by God and <u>profitable for teaching, for reproof, for correction, and for training in righteousness</u>, that the man of God may be complete, equipped for every good work. 2 Timothy 3:16

<u>Do not be yoked together with unbelievers</u>. For what do righteousness and wickedness have in common? Or what fellowship can light have with darkness? 2 Corinthians 6:14

The wicked plot against the righteous and gnash their teeth at them; but the Lord laughs at the wicked, for He knows their day is coming. The wicked draw the sword and bend the bow to bring down the poor and needy, to slay those whose ways are upright.

But their swords will pierce their own hearts, and their bows will be broken. <u>Better the little that the righteous have than the wealth of many wicked</u>; for the power of the wicked will be broken, but the LORD upholds the righteous. Psalm 37:12-17

I have been crucified with Christ and <u>I no longer live</u>, but Christ lives in me. The life I now live in the body, I live by faith in the Son of God, who loved me and gave Himself for me. Galatians 2:20

The Tao Te Ching - Chapter 21

Hole heart him to allow <u>only the Way to follow</u>.
孔德之容惟道是从。

The Way him create creature only, seemingly because confused. 道之為物惟，恍惟惚。
Suddenly! Absent minded! 惚兮！恍兮！
Him center occupy figure. 其中有象。
Absent minded! Abruptly! Him attain good harvest creature. 恍兮！惚兮！其中有物。

Obscure! Dark! His center exist spirit.
窈兮！冥兮！其中有精。

That energy very real. 其精甚真。
His within to have evidence. 其中有信。

Self ancient and modern, his fame not leave because read multitude begin. 自古及今，其名不去以閱众甫。

We who believe, understand multitude great, him official begin? 吾何以知众甫，之状哉？

<u>Believe this</u>. 以此。

The Holy Bible

Be sober, be vigilant; because your adversary the devil, as a roaring lion, walketh about, <u>seeking whom he may devour</u>: Whom resist stedfast in the faith, knowing that the same afflictions are accomplished in your brethren that are in the world.
1 Peter 5:8-9

We know that anyone born of God does not continue to sin; the One who was born of God keeps them safe, and the evil one cannot harm them.

We know that we are children of God, and that the whole world is under the control of the evil one. We know also that the Son of God has come and has given us understanding, so that we may know him who is true. And we are in him who is true by being in his Son Jesus Christ. He is the true God and eternal life.
1 John 5:18-20

If we receive the witness of men, the witness of God is greater: for this is the witness of God which He hath testified of his Son.

He that believeth on the Son of God hath the witness in himself: he that believeth not God hath made him a liar; because he believeth not the record that God gave of his Son.

<u>And this is the record</u>, that God hath given to us eternal life, and this life is in his Son. He that hath the Son hath life; and he that hath not the Son of God hath not life.
1 John 5:9-12

The Tao Te Ching - Chapter 22

<u>Bent follow whole</u>, crooked follow upright, depression follow surplus, ragged follow fresh.
曲則全，枉則直，洼則盈，敝則新。

Lack rule, proud many to follow confused.
少則，得多則惑。

<u>This according to sage man</u>, cherish one to become god rule.
是以圣人，抱一爲天下式。

Not oneself see reason clear; <u>not oneself cause manifest</u>.
不自见故明；不自是故彰。

<u>Not oneself fell, reason there is work</u>; Not oneself. Pity happening regularly. 不自伐，故有功；不自。矜故长。

<u>Man alone not fight</u>. Hence, god below there is none who can give him fight. 夫唯不争。 故，天下莫能与之争。

Ancient him place says: wrong follow finished. **How can that be empty words!** Honest all and return him.
古之所謂：曲則全者。 豈虛言哉！ 誠全而归之。

The Holy Bible

That is, <u>in Christ, God was reconciling the world to Himself</u>, <u>not counting their trespasses against them</u>, and He has committed the message of reconciliation to us. Therefore, we are ambassadors for Christ, certain that God is appealing through us. We plead on Christ's behalf, "Be reconciled to God."
2 Corinthians 5:19-20

For the grace of God that bringeth salvation hath appeared to all men, teaching us that, denying ungodliness and worldly lusts, we should live soberly, righteously, and Godly, in this present world;
Titus 2:11-12

<u>And we impart this in words not taught by human wisdom but taught by the Spirit</u>, interpreting spiritual truths to those who are spiritual. 1 Corinthians 2:13

Wherefore, <u>as by one man sin entered into the world</u>, and death by sin; and so death passed upon all men, for that all have sinned:
Romans 5:12

<u>By the sweat of your brow</u> you will eat your food until you return to the ground, since from it you were taken; for dust you are and to dust you will return. Genesis 3:19

Jesus answered, "It is written: '<u>Man shall not live on bread alone</u>, but on every word that comes from the mouth of God.'"
Matthew 4:4

Which is easier: to say, 'Your sins are forgiven,' or to say, 'Get up and walk'? Luke 5:23

The Tao Te Ching - Chapter 23

<u>Rare words oneself true</u>. 希言自然。

Hence, float <u>custom</u> not end facing sudden rain, not end sun.
故,飄风不終朝驟雨,不終日。

Who serve as this person? Heaven earth.
孰為此者? 天地。

Heaven earth to value no energy long time, but moreover in regard to man? 天地尚不能久,而況于人乎?

Hence, <u>follow serve in the Way</u>, he who <u>similar to The Way</u>.
故,从事于道,者同于道。

<u>Morals similar in character</u>. Fail similar to lose.
德者同于德。 失者同于失。

Together in principle, person the Way also happy gain him.
同于道,者道亦樂得之。

Together in morality, person heart also cheerfully permit him.
同于德,者德亦樂得之。

Together in fail, person fail at happy contented him.
同于失,者失于樂得之。

<u>Trust not enough</u>, **have no trust here**.
信不足焉,有不信焉。

The Holy Bible

The more you talk, the more you are likely to sin. <u>If you are wise, you will keep quiet.</u>   Proverbs 10:19

See to it that no one takes you captive through hollow and deceptive philosophy, which depends on <u>human tradition</u> and the elemental spiritual forces of this world rather than on Christ.   Colossians 2:8

So then, brothers and sisters, stand firm and hold fast to the teachings we passed on to you, whether by word of mouth or by letter.   2 Thessalonians 2:15

Take heed to yourselves, that your heart <u>be not deceived</u>, and ye turn aside, <u>and serve other gods</u>, and worship them.   Deuteronomy 11:16

<u>There is a way that seems right to a man, but its end is the way to death</u>. Even in laughter the heart may ache, and the end of joy may be grief.   Proverbs 14:12-13

Jesus answered, "**I am the way and the truth and the life.** No one comes to the Father except through Me".   John 14:6

<u>Trust in the LORD </u>with all your heart and lean not on your own understanding;   Proverbs 3:5

He who trusts in his own heart is a fool, But he who walks wisely will be delivered.   Proverbs 28:26

The Tao Te Ching - Chapter 24

<u>Look forward to that which not exist</u>; Carry those who do not walk. 企者不立；跨者不行。

Oneself see those who unclear; 自见者不明；
Naturally, this <u>those who not manifest</u>. 自，是者不彰。
Since fall, person no merit. 自伐，者无功。
Self pity person, not forever. 自矜者，不长。

They exist the Way also say; <u>excess food superfluous form</u>. 其在道也曰；余食赘形。

<u>Matter perhaps of evil</u>, him cause to exist <u>the Way person not live</u>. 物或惡，之故有道者不处。

The Holy Bible

But the day of the Lord will come as a thief in the night; in the which the heavens shall pass away with a great noise, and the elements shall melt with fervent heat, the earth also and the works that are therein shall be burned up. Seeing then that all these things shall be dissolved, what manner of persons ought ye to be in all holy conversation and godliness, <u>Looking for and hasting unto the coming of the day of God</u>, wherein the heavens being on fire shall be dissolved, and the elements shall melt with fervent heat? Nevertheless we, according to his promise, look for new heavens and a new earth, wherein dwelleth righteousness.
2 Peter 3:10-13

The fruit of the righteous is a tree of life, and whoever captures souls is wise. If the righteous is repaid on earth, how much more the wicked and the sinner!   Proverbs 11:30-31

Set your affection on things above, not on things on the earth. For ye are dead, and <u>your life is hid with Christ in God</u>. When Christ, who is our life, shall appear, then shall ye also appear with him in glory.   Colossians 3:2-4

Their end is destruction, <u>their god is their belly</u>, and they glory in their shame, with minds set on earthly things.
Philippians 3:19

<u>Turn away from evil</u> and do good, and <u>abide forever</u>.
Psalm 37:27

The Tao Te Ching - Chapter 25

Have matter <u>confused</u> turn into <u>first heaven and earth life</u>.
有物混成先天地生。

Silent! Empty! Alone stand not changed, all okay, and no danger. Can believe earth is mother.
寂兮！寥兮！独立不改，周行，而不殆。 可以為天下母。

<u>We not know his name</u>, <u>powerful word called the Way</u>.
吾不知其名，强字之曰道。

<u>Powerful become his name called great</u>. 强為之名曰大。

Great name die, die name profound, distant name return.
大曰逝，逝曰遠，遠曰反。

Hence, the Way great, heaven great, earth great, man also great. 故道大，天大，地大，人亦大。
Region center exist four great, yet king have his one here.
域中有四大，而人居其一焉。

Man follow earth, earth follows heaven, heaven follows God, <u>the Way follows oneself truth</u>.
人法地，地法天，天法道， 道法自然。

The Holy Bible

Why should you be like <u>a man confused</u>, like a mighty warrior who cannot save? Yet you, O LORD, are in the midst of us, and we are called by your name; do not leave us.   Jeremiah 14:9

Then God said, "Let us make mankind in our image, in our likeness, so that they may rule over the fish in the sea and the birds in the sky, over the livestock and all the wild animals, and over all the creatures that move along the ground."   Genesis 1:26

Then I saw a new heaven and a new earth, for <u>the first heaven and the first earth</u> had passed away, and the sea was no more.   Revelation 21:1

For as I passed along and observed the objects of your worship, I found also an altar with this inscription, '<u>To the unknown god</u>.' What therefore you worship as unknown, this I proclaim to you.   Acts 17:23

Jesus answered, "<u>I am the way</u> and the truth and the life. No one comes to the Father except through me".   John 14:16

For I know that <u>the LORD is great</u>, and that our Lord is above all gods.   Psalm 135:5

Jesus said to them, "I am the bread of life; he who comes to Me will not hunger, and he who believes in Me will never thirst. But I said to you that you have seen Me, and yet do not believe".   John 6:35-36

The Spirit clearly says that in later times some will abandon the faith and <u>follow deceiving spirits and things taught by demons</u>.   1 Timothy 4:1

The Tao Te Ching - Chapter 26

Heavy act as light root, still act as impatient ruler.
重為輕根,靜為躁君。

That because ruler end day travel, not leave easy weight.
是以君子終日行,不离輕重。

Though there is honor to behold, comfort reside surpass however. 虽有荣觀,燕处超然。

Endure what ten thousand chariot it master, and use body light god below.
奈何万乘之主,而以身輕天下。

Easy to imitate leave root. Impatient rule, leave ruler.
輕則失根。 躁則,失君。

The Holy Bible

You were taught, with regard to your former way of life, to put off your old self, which is being corrupted by its deceitful desires;
Ephesians 4:22

Do not conform to the pattern of this world, but be transformed by the renewing of your mind. Then you will be able to test and approve what God's will is--his good, pleasing and perfect will.
Romans 12:2

I am the vine, ye are the branches: He that abideth in me, and I in him, the same bringeth forth much fruit: for without me ye can do nothing.
John 15:5

I Jesus have sent mine angel to testify unto you these things in the churches. I am the root and the offspring of David, and the bright and morning star. And the Spirit and the bride say, Come. And let him that heareth say, Come. And let him that is athirst come. And whosoever will, let him take the water of life freely.

For I testify unto every man that heareth the words of the prophecy of this book, If any man shall add unto these things, God shall add unto him the plagues that are written in this book:

And if any man shall take away from the words of the book of this prophecy, God shall take away his part out of the book of life, and out of the holy city, and from the things which are written in this book.
Revelation 22:16-19

The Tao Te Ching - Chapter 27

<u>Good move not having wheel ruts to trace</u>.
善行无轍迹。

<u>Good talk not having fault blame</u>. 善言无瑕謫。

Good count not use counter plan. 善数不用籌策。

Good close without shut door lock, yet not able to open.
善閉无關楗，而不可開。

Good tie without rope restrain, yet no can untie.
善結无繩約，而不可解。

That according to sage man. 是以圣人。

Often good <u>rescue</u> man, reason not abandon man.
常善救人，故无弃人。

Often good rescue creature, reason not abandon creature.
常善救物，故无弃物。

This means attack bright. 是謂襲明。

Hence, good man not good man him Master.
故，善人者不善人之师。

Not good man, person good people him support.
不善人，者善人之資。

Not value their teacher, not love his support even though wisdom great, confused. 不貴其师，不愛其資虽智大，迷。

This means ask clever. 是謂要妙。

The Holy Bible

<u>Be imitators of me</u>, as I am of Christ. Now I commend you because you remember me in everything and maintain the traditions even as I delivered them to you. 1 Corinthians 11:1-2

For to this you have been called, because Christ also suffered for you, leaving you an example, **so that you might follow in His steps**. 1 Peter 2:21

<u>A good man out of the good treasure of the heart bringeth forth good things</u>: and an evil man out of the evil treasure bringeth forth evil things. Matthew 12:35

For it is God who works in you, both to will and to work for His good pleasure. Philippians 2:13

For by grace <u>you have been saved</u> through faith. And this is not your own doing; it is the gift of God, not a result of works, so that no one may boast. For we are his workmanship, created in Christ Jesus for good works, which God prepared beforehand, that we should walk in them. Ephesians 2:8-10

In everything set them an example by doing what is good. In your teaching show integrity, seriousness and soundness of speech that cannot be condemned, so that those who oppose you may be ashamed because they have nothing bad to say about us. Titus 2:7-8

Let your light shine before men in such a way that they may see your good works, and glorify your Father who is in heaven. Matthew 5:16

The Tao Te Ching - Chapter 28

<u>Know its male, defend its female</u>, serve as all under heaven small stream. 知其雄，守其雌，為天下溪。

Serve as all under heaven small stream, always virtue not leave, again return to infant son.
為天下溪，常德不离，复归于婴儿。

<u>Know its white, defend its black</u>, named all under heaven rule, become all under heaven system.
知其白，守其黑，為天下式，為天下式。

Common heart not change, repeatedly return to without extreme.
常德不忒，复归于无极。

Know its honor, defend its disgrace, serve as all under heaven valley. 知其荣，守其辱，為天下谷。

Serving as all heaven under valley, always virtue therefore full, again return to simple. 為天下谷，常德乃足，复归于朴。

Simple disperse regulation serve as instrument, <u>sage man use this method become public elder</u>.
朴散 則為器，圣人用之則為官长。

<u>Death</u> many establish, not divide. 故大制，不割。

The Holy Bible

<u>No man can serve two masters</u>: for either he will hate the one, and love the other; or else he will hold to the one, and despise the other. Ye cannot serve God and mammon.　　　　　Mark 6:24

And Jesus knew their thoughts, and said unto them, Every <u>kingdom divided against itself is brought to desolation</u>; and every city or house divided against itself shall not stand: And if Satan cast out Satan, he is divided against himself; how shall then his kingdom stand?

And if I by Beelzebub cast out devils, by whom do your children cast them out? therefore they shall be your judges. But if I cast out devils by the Spirit of God, then the kingdom of God is come unto you.　　　　　Matthew 12:25-28

Jesus called them together and said, "You know that the rulers of the Gentiles lord it over them, and their high officials exercise authority over them. Not so with you. Instead, <u>whoever wants to become great among you must be your servant</u>, and whoever wants to be first must be your slave-- just as the Son of Man did not come to be served, but to serve, and to give his life as a ransom for many."　　　　　Matthew 20:25-28

Whoever is not with me is against me, and whoever does not gather with me scatters.　　　　　Matthew 12:30

I call heaven and earth to record this day against you, that <u>I have set before you life and death</u>, blessing and cursing: therefore choose life, that both thou and thy seed may live:
　　　　　Deuteronomy 30:19

The Tao Te Ching - Chapter 29

<u>Use desire capture all under heaven and serve him. We catch sight of their not satisfied end.</u>
將欲取天下而為之。 吾見其不得已。

All under heaven instrument, **not possible to serve either.**
天下神器，不可為也。

Govern those who defeated, <u>these execute those who neglect him</u>. 為者敗，之執者失之。

Man matter perhaps to walk, **perhaps to follow**, perhaps snort, perhaps boast, perhaps powerful, perhaps to win, perhaps **fail**, perhaps **destroy**.
夫物或行，或隨，或歔，或吹，或強，或羸，或挫，或隳。

That because of sage man remove extreme, remove excessive, remove extravagant. 是以圣人去甚，去奢，去泰。

The Holy Bible

Let no man say when he is tempted, I am tempted of God: for God cannot be tempted with evil, neither tempteth he any man: But every man is tempted, when he is drawn away of his own lust, and enticed. <u>Then when lust hath conceived, it bringeth forth sin: and sin, when it is finished, **bringeth forth death**</u>.   James 1:13-15

Watch and pray, that ye enter not into temptation: **the spirit indeed is willing, but the flesh is weak.**   Matthew 26:41

Submit yourselves, then, to God. Resist the devil, and he will flee from you.   James 4:7

They will put you out of the synagogue; in fact, the time is coming when <u>anyone who kills you will think they are offering a service to God</u>.   John 16:2

For God did not send the Son into the world to judge the world, but that the world might be saved through Him. He who believes in Him is not judged; he who does not believe has been judged already, because he has not believed in the name of the only begotten Son of God".   John 3:17-18

And the devil, who deceived them, was thrown into the lake of burning sulfur, where the beast and the false prophet had been thrown. They will be tormented day and night for ever and ever.   Revelation 10:20

But God chose the foolish things of the world to shame the wise; God chose the weak things of the world to shame the strong.   1 Corinthians 1:27

The Tao Te Ching - Chapter 30

Use the Way assist people to master <u>those who not use military force</u>. All under heaven his work good pay back.
以道佐人主者不以兵強。 天下其事好还。

Master this place to dwell, brambles thorn bushes to give birth to him. 师之所处，荆棘生焉。

Army him future, certainly to be bad year.
軍之后，必有凶年。

<u>Good have fruit</u>, but stop, <u>not to dare because capture powerful</u>. 善有果，而已，不敢以取強。

Fruit, but without pity. 果，而勿矜。

Fruit, yet don't strike. 果，而勿伐。

Fruit, but without proud. 果，而勿驕。

Fruit, yet not satisfied afterwards. 果，而不得已。

Fruit, yet don't strive. 果，而勿強。

Thing robust mimic aged, this called not the Way.
物壯則老，是謂不道。

<u>Not of the Way soon end</u>. 不道早已。

The Holy Bible

Our God, will you not judge them? For <u>we have no power to face this vast army that is attacking us</u>. We do not know what to do, but our eyes are on you.   2 Chronicles 20

And the third angel poured out his vial upon the rivers and fountains of waters; and they became blood. And I heard the angel of the waters say, Thou art righteous, O Lord, which art, and wast, and shalt be, because thou hast judged thus.

For they have shed the blood of saints and prophets, and thou hast given them blood to drink; for they are worthy.   Revelation 16:4-6

<u>No good tree bears **bad fruit**, nor does a bad tree bear **good fruit**</u>. Each tree is recognized by its own fruit. People do not pick figs from thornbushes, or grapes from briers. The good person out of the good treasure of his heart produces good, <u>and the evil person out of his evil treasure produces evil</u>, for out of the abundance of the heart his mouth speaks.   Luke 6:43-45

When the Son of man shall come in his glory, and all the holy angels with him, then shall he sit upon the throne of his glory:
And before him shall be gathered all nations: and he shall separate them one from another, as a shepherd divideth his sheep from the goats: And he shall set the **sheep on his right** hand, but the **goats on the left**.   Matthew 25:31-34

For the great day of his wrath is come; and who shall be able to stand?   Revelation 6:17
<u>The God of peace will soon crush Satan</u> under your feet.
The grace of our Lord Jesus be with you.   Romans 16:20

The Tao Te Ching - Chapter 31

Man good soldier those who not good, <u>him instrument</u>.
夫佳兵者不祥，之器。
Creature <u>confuse</u> bad these. 物或惡之。

Hence, hold onto the Way <u>he who not judge</u>.
故有道者不處。

A moral man normal rule costly unorthodox, <u>use soldiers to follow costly right</u>. 君子居則貴左，用兵則貴右。

Soldiers those who not good, him instrument.
兵者不祥，之器。

<u>Oppose a moral man</u>, these instruments not proud end, but use these. **Peaceful weak** act as superior.
非君子，之器不得已，而用之。 恬淡為上。

Victory but not beautiful, yet beautiful this person. This musical instrument kill men.
勝而不美，而美之者。 是樂殺人。

Men musical instrument kill people, follow not able to obtain the will God heaven under! 夫樂殺人者，則不可得志于天下矣！

Good work still left, ominous work still right.
吉事尚左，凶事尚右。

Slanting help soldiers live unorthodox, superior follow soldiers live right. 偏將居軍左，上將軍居右。
Say according to mourning, gift deal with him.
言以喪，礼处之。

<u>Murder people these masses,</u> so as to sadness, to grieve, to sob him. Fight victorious so as to lose gift to live him.
殺人之众，以悲，哀，泣之。 战胜以礼处之。

The Holy Bible

He who is not with Me is against Me; and he who does not gather with Me <u>scatters</u>.   Matthew 12:30

For God is not the author of <u>confusion</u>, but of peace, as in all churches of the saints.   1 Corinthians 14:33

"<u>I the LORD search the heart and examine the mind, to reward each person according to their conduct, according to what their deeds deserve</u>."   Jeremiah 17:10

<u>No weapon that is fashioned against you shall succeed</u>, and you shall confute every tongue that rises against you in judgment. This is the heritage of the servants of the Lord and their vindication from Me, declares the Lord.   Isaiah 54:17

"But I say to you, love your enemies and <u>pray for those who persecute you</u>"   Matthew 5:44

"For My hand made all these things, Thus all these things came into being," declares the LORD. " But to this one I will look, **To him who is humble and contrite of spirit, and who trembles at My word**. But he who kills an ox is like one who slays a man; He who sacrifices a lamb is like the one who breaks a dog's neck; He who offers a grain offering is like one who offers swine's blood; He who burns incense is like the one who blesses an idol.

<u>As they have chosen their own ways</u>, And their soul delights in their abominations, So I will choose their punishments And will bring on them what they dread. Because I called, but no one answered; I spoke, but they did not listen. And <u>they did evil in My sight</u> and chose that in which I did not delight."   Isaiah 66:2-4

<u>You shall not murder</u>.   Exodus 20:13

The Tao Te Ching - Chapter 32

<u>The Way constant without name</u>. Simple though small, heaven below there is none who able minister also.
道常无名。 朴虽小，天下莫能臣也。

Marquis <u>king</u> seem able to guard him, ten thousand thing prepared since visitor. 侯王若能守之，万物将自賓。

Heaven earth together unite, reason descend sweet exposed, <u>people do not this cause</u>, but oneself equal.
天地相合，以降甘露，民莫之令，而自均。

Begin overpower, posses title, famous also since good harvest. 始制，有名，名亦既有。

Men just <u>use knowledge</u> detain. Understand detain place have not danger. 夫亦将知止。 知止可以不殆。

Example the Way, him exist all under heaven, <u>Jew</u> <u>river</u> valley. 譬道，之在天下，犹川谷。

Him in river <u>sea</u>. 之于江海。

The Holy Bible

And this is life eternal, <u>that they might know thee the only true God, and **Jesus Christ**</u>, whom thou hast sent. John 17:3

It is the glory of God to conceal a thing: but <u>the honour of kings is to search out a matter</u>. Proverbs 25:2

You will seek me and find me when you seek me with all your heart. Jeremiah 29:13

<u>He who rejects Me, and does not receive My words, has that which judges him— the word that I have spoken will judge him in the last day</u>. John 12:48

<u>The fear of the LORD is the beginning of knowledge</u>, but fools despise wisdom and instruction. Proverbs 1:7

"Are you the king of the <u>Jews</u>?" asked Pilate. "You have said so," Jesus replied. Mark 15:2

Whoever believes in me, as the Scripture has said, 'Out of his heart will flow <u>rivers of living water</u>.'" John 7:38

Then he showed me a **river of the water of life**, clear as crystal, coming from the throne of God and of the Lamb. Revelation 22:1

And I stood upon the sand of the sea, and saw <u>a beast rise up out of the **sea**</u>, having seven heads and ten horns, and upon his horns ten crowns, and upon his heads the name of blasphemy. Revelation 13:1

The Tao Te Ching - Chapter 33

<u>Know people person knowledge, self know person clear.</u>
知人者智，自知者明。

<u>Victorious</u> people person have power. 胜人者有力。
<u>Oneself able</u> to bear person powerful. 自胜者强。
Know enough, person rich. 知足，者富。

<u>Powerful</u> carry out, person possess the will. 强行，者有志。
Not to leave his place person for a long time. 不失其所者久。

<u>Death and not lose persons life.</u> 死而不亡者寿。

The Holy Bible

For <u>the foolishness of God is wiser than human wisdom</u>, and the weakness of God is stronger than human strength.
1 Corinthians 1:25

Do you not know that in a race all the runners run, but only one <u>gets the prize</u>? Run in such a way as to get the prize.

Everyone who competes in the games goes into strict training. <u>They do it to get a crown that will not last, but we do it to get a crown that will last forever</u>. Therefore I do not run like someone running aimlessly; I do not fight like a boxer beating the air. No, I strike a blow to my body and make it my slave so that after I have preached to others, I myself will not be disqualified for the prize.
1 Corinthians 9:24-27

Then Jesus sent the multitude away, and went into the house: and his disciples came unto him, saying, Declare unto us the parable of the tares of the field.

He answered and said unto them, He that soweth the good seed is the Son of man; The field is the world; the good seed are the children of the kingdom; but the tares are the children of the wicked one;

The enemy that sowed them is <u>the devil</u>; the harvest is the end of the world; and the reapers are the angels.

As therefore the tares are gathered and burned in the fire; so shall it be in the end of this world. The Son of man shall send forth his angels, and they shall gather out of his kingdom all things that offend, and them which do iniquity;

And shall cast them into a furnace of fire: there shall be wailing and gnashing of teeth. Then shall the righteous shine forth as the sun in the kingdom of their Father. Who hath ears to hear, let him hear.
Matthew 13:36-43

<u>Whoever believes in him should not perish but have eternal life</u>.
John 3:16

The Tao Te Ching - Chapter 34

The Great Way <u>flood</u>! He able to **left right**.
大道泛兮！其可左右。

Ten thousand things rely on him so as to give birth, but no diction. 万物恃之以生，而不辞。

Meritorious become, <u>yet no name exists</u>.
功成，而不名有。

<u>Clothes to raise</u> ten thousand things, yet not act as master.
衣養万物，而不為主。

Constant <u>without desire</u> befits name in regard to tiny.
常无欲可名於小。

Ten thousand things return where, yet not for master, befits name to become great. 万物归焉，而不為主，可名為大。

<u>Because his death</u>, no oneself become great, reason energy succeed his great. 以其終，不自為大，故能成其大。

The Holy Bible

And Noah and his sons and his wife and his sons' wives entered the ark to escape the waters of the <u>flood</u>.
Genesis 7:7

That ye may be the children of your Father which is in heaven: for he maketh his sun to rise on the evil and on the good, <u>and sendeth rain on **the just and on the unjust**</u>. That ye may be the children of your Father which is in heaven: for he maketh his sun to rise on the evil and on the good, and sendeth rain on the just and on the unjust.
Matthew 5:45-46

God said to Moses, "<u>I AM WHO I AM</u>. This is what you are to say to the Israelites: 'I AM has sent me to you.'"
Exodus 3:14

And He is not served by human hands, as if He needed anything. Rather, <u>He himself gives everyone life and breath **and everything else**</u>.
Acts 17:25

Look at the birds of the air; they do not sow or reap or store away in barns, and yet your heavenly Father feeds them. Are you not much more valuable than they?
Matthew 6:26

Follow the way of love and <u>eagerly desire</u> gifts of the Spirit, especially prophecy.
1 Corinthians 14:1

Once you were alienated from God and were enemies in your minds because of your evil behavior. But now he has reconciled you by <u>Christ's physical body through death</u> to present you holy in his sight, without blemish and free from accusation.
Colossians 1:21-22

And Pilate wrote a title, and put it on the cross. And the writing was: Jesus Of Nazareth The King Of The Jews.
John 19:19

The Tao Te Ching - Chapter 35

Execute great appearance, heaven to go down <u>past</u>.
执大象，天下往。

Past, yet not cause trouble to pacify peaceful, too.
往，而不害安平，太。

Happy to give cakes to get along, visitor only.
與与餌，过客止。

The Way him <u>exit mouth</u> tasteless?
道之出口淡乎？
Him not delicacy. 其无味。

<u>Watch him not be sufficient to appear</u>. 视之不足见。

<u>Listen him not not be sufficient to hear</u>. 听之不足闻。

Use him to not be enough both. 用之不足既。

The Holy Bible

I have fought the good fight, I have finished the course, I have kept the faith; <u>in the future</u> there is laid up for me the crown of righteousness, which the Lord, the righteous Judge, will award to me on that day; and not only to me, but also to all who have loved His appearing.   2 Timothy 4:7-8

A greedy man stirs up strife, but the one who trusts in the LORD will be enriched.   Proverbs 28:25

After Jesus called the crowd to Him, He said to them, "Hear and understand. "It is not what enters into the mouth that defiles the man, but what proceeds <u>out of the mouth</u>, this defiles the man."

And when he was alone, they that were about him with the twelve asked of him the parable.   Matthew 15:10-11

And he said unto them, Unto you it is given to know the mystery of the kingdom of God: but unto them that are without, all these things are done in parables: <u>That seeing they may see, and not perceive; and hearing they may hear, and not understand</u>; lest at any time they should be converted, and their sins should be forgiven them. And he said unto them, Know ye not this parable? and how then will ye know all parables?

The sower soweth the word. And these are they by the way side, where the word is sown; but when they have heard, <u>Satan cometh immediately, and taketh away the word that was sown in their hearts</u>. And these are they likewise which are sown on stony ground; who, when they have heard the word, immediately receive it with gladness; And have no root in themselves, and so endure but for a time: afterward, when affliction or persecution ariseth for the word's sake, immediately they are offended.   Mark 4:10-17

The Tao Te Ching - Chapter 36

To use desire, <u>inhale</u> him, certainly solid <u>open to him</u>.
将欲,歙之,必固張之。

<u>Use desire</u> weak him, certainly solid <u>powerful him</u>.
将欲弱之,必固强之。
To use desire discard him, certainly solid advocate him.
将欲廢之,必固兴之。
To use desire rob him, certainly solid give him.
将欲取之,必固与之。

That called tiny clear. 是謂微明。

Soft weak <u>victory</u> firm power. 柔弱胜剛強。

Fish not able take off from abyss,
country him sharp instruments <u>not able to show people</u>.
鱼不可脱于渊,国之利器不可以示人。

The Holy Bible

Submit yourselves therefore to God. <u>Resist the devil</u>, and he will flee from you.   James 4:7

And you were dead in your trespasses and sins, in which you formerly walked according to the course of this world, according to the prince of <u>the power of the air</u>, of the spirit that is now working in the sons of disobedience.   Ephesians 2:1-2

Take delight in the LORD, and <u>he will give you the desires of your heart</u>.   Psalm 37:4

This is the confidence we have in approaching God: that if we ask anything according to his will, He hears us.   1 John 5:14

You are from God, little children, and have overcome them; because **greater is He who is in you than he who is in the world**.   1 John 4:4

The sting of death is sin, and the power of sin is the law. But thanks be to God! <u>He gives us the victory</u> through our Lord Jesus Christ.

Therefore, my dear brothers and sisters, stand firm. **Let nothing move you**. Always give yourselves fully to the work of the Lord, because you know that your labor in the Lord is not in vain.   1 Corinthians 15:56-58

<u>For there is nothing hidden that will not be disclosed</u>, and nothing concealed that will not be known or brought out into the open.   Luke 8:17

The Tao Te Ching - Chapter 37

The Way often not do, yet without not do.
道常无為，而无不為。

Marquis King great ability defend him, ten thousand things carry out <u>natural change</u>.
侯王若能守之，万物將自化。

Change, yet <u>desire</u> arise. 化，而欲作。

I carry out suppress these, so as to not have reputation him simple. 吾將鎮之，以无名之朴。

Without fame, <u>him simple solider</u> also execute without desire.
无名，之朴夫亦將无欲。

<u>Not have desire</u> reason still, all under heaven use oneself settle. 不欲以静，天下將自定。

The Holy Bible

Behold, I stand at the door and knock; if anyone hears My voice and opens the door, I will come in to him and will dine with him, and he with Me. Revelation 3:20

Therefore I urge you, brethren, by the mercies of God, to present your bodies a living and holy sacrifice, acceptable to God, which is your spiritual service of worship. And do not be conformed to this world, but <u>be transformed by the renewing of your mind</u>, so that you may prove what the will of God is, that which is good and acceptable and perfect. Romans 12:2

No <u>temptation</u> has overtaken you except what is common to mankind. And God is faithful; he will not let you be tempted beyond what you can bear. But when you are tempted, he will also provide a way out so that you can endure it. 1 Corinthians 10:13

And <u>the devil</u>, who deceived them, was thrown into the lake of burning sulfur, where the beast and the false prophet had been thrown. They will be tormented day and night for ever and ever. Revelation 20:10

<u>The demons begged</u> Jesus, "Send us among the pigs; allow us to go into them."

He gave them permission, and the impure spirits came out and went into the pigs. The herd, about two thousand in number, rushed down the steep bank into the lake and were drowned. Mark 5:12-13

The Tao Te Ching - Chapter 38

<u>Superior virtue not morality</u>, is because exist character.
上德不德，是以有德。

Inferior virtue not lose morality, that use without character.
下德不失德，是以无德。

Superior virtue without do, yet not have believe name.
上德无為，而无以為。

Inferior virtue name him, but **have believe name**.
下德无為，而有以為。

<u>Superior humaneness govern him</u>, yet not have change.
上仁為之，而无以為。

Superior righteousness govern him, and have believe name.
上义為之，而有以為。

Superior courtesy govern him, but is not this must rule. <u>Take by force arm and throw him</u>.
上礼為之，而莫之以應。 則攘臂而扔之。

Hence, lose the Way and afterward morality. 故失道而后德。
Lose morality and afterward humaneness. 失德而后仁。
Lose humaneness and afterward righteousness. 失仁而后义。
<u>Lose righteousness</u> and afterward rites. 失义而后礼。

Mans etiquette, person loyal to believe him. Weak but confusion him leader. 夫礼者忠信之，薄而乱之首。

<u>Before knowledge</u>, person the Way him flowery, but stupid it begin. 前識者，道之华而愚之始。

That because great man reside his thick, not dwell his thin. 是以大丈夫，处其厚，不居其薄。

Dwell his <u>truth</u>, not reside his flowery. 处其实，不居其华。
Hence, remove that, take this. 故，去彼，取此。

The Holy Bible

For this very reason, make every effort to <u>supplement your faith with virtue</u>, and virtue with knowledge, and knowledge with self-control, and self-control with steadfastness, and steadfastness with godliness, and godliness with brotherly affection, and brotherly affection with love.

For if these qualities are yours and are increasing, they keep you from being ineffective or unfruitful in the knowledge of our Lord Jesus Christ. 2 Peter 1:5-8

<u>There is a way that appears to be right</u>, but in the end it leads to death. Even in laughter the heart may ache, and rejoicing may end in grief. The faithless will be fully repaid for their ways, and the good rewarded for theirs. The simple believe anything, but the prudent give thought to their steps.

The wise fear the LORD and shun evil, <u>but a fool is hotheaded and yet feels secure.</u> Proverbs 14:12-16

God made him who had no sin to be sin for us, so that in him we might <u>become the righteousness</u> of God. 2 Corinthians 5:21

The heart of the discerning <u>acquires knowledge</u>, for the ears of the wise seek it out. Proverbs 18:15

My people are destroyed for lack of knowledge. Because you have rejected knowledge, I also will reject you from being My priest. Since you have forgotten the law of your God, I also will forget your children. Hosea 4:6

Wherefore putting away lying, speak every man <u>truth</u> with his neighbour: for we are members one of another. Ephesians 4:25

The Tao Te Ching - Chapter 39

<u>Past him get one person</u>. 昔之得一者。
<u>God get one became clear</u>. 天得一以清。
Earth get one became peaceful. 地得一以宁。
God get one became spirit. 神得一以灵。
Valley get one became full. 谷得一以盈。

Ten thousand things <u>get one</u>, became life. 万物得一，以生。

Marquis King get one, use make all under heaven virtuous. He deliver this. 侯王得一，以為天下貞。 其致之。

God without use clear will **fear** rend.
天无以清将恐裂。

Earth without use peaceful, will **fear** abolish.
地无以宁，将恐廢。

God without use departed soul, will **fear** stop.
神无以灵，将恐歇。

Valley without use full will fear stop. Ten thousand things without use life, will fear extinguish.
谷无以盈将恐竭。 万物无以生，将恐滅。

Marquis King without use chaste will fear fall.
侯王无以貞将恐蹶。

Hence, expensive to use inexpensive origin. High to use low foundation. 故，貴以為本。 高以下為基。

This use Marquis King oneself name modestly, widowed, not valley. 是以侯王自称孤，寡，不谷。

This wrong cause worthless become <u>origin evil</u>. No?
此非以賤為本邪。 非乎？

Until reputation not reputation, no desire jade like stone. Jade like stone as good as gem kind of necklace.
至譽无譽，不欲琭。 琭如玉珞。

Kind of necklace comparable to rock. 珞如石。

The Holy Bible

Just as <u>people are destined to die once</u>, and after that to face judgment, so <u>Christ was sacrificed once</u> to take away the sins of many; and he will appear a second time, not to bear sin, but to bring salvation to those who are waiting for him.
Hebrews 9:27-28

As water reflects the face, so <u>one's life</u> reflects the heart. Death and Destruction are **never satisfied**, and neither are human eyes. The crucible for silver and the furnace for gold, but people are tested by their praise. Proverbs 27:19

<u>There is no **fear** in love</u>. But perfect love drives out fear, because fear has to do with punishment. The one who fears is not made perfect in love. 1 John 4:18

<u>The **fear** of the Lord leads to life</u>, and whoever has it rests **satisfied**; he will not be visited by harm. Proverbs 19:23

For thus the LORD spoke to me with mighty power and instructed me not to walk in the way of this people, saying, "You are not to say, 'It is a conspiracy!' In regard to all that this people call a conspiracy, And <u>you are not to **fear** what they fear</u> or be in dread of it. "It is the LORD of hosts whom you should regard as holy. And He shall be your fear, And He shall be your dread.
Isaiah 8:11-13

For <u>rebellion is like the sin of divination</u>, and arrogance like the evil of idolatry. Because you have rejected the word of the LORD, He has rejected you as king. 1 Samuel 15:13

Grace be to you and peace from God the Father, and from our Lord Jesus Christ, Who gave himself for our sins, that he might deliver us from this present evil world, according to the will of God and our Father: To whom be glory for ever and ever. Amen.
Galatians 1:3-5

The Tao Te Ching - Chapter 40

<u>Anti-Person</u> the Way him to act. 反者道之动。

Weak person the Way him to use. 弱者道之用。

All under heaven ten thousand <u>things life exist</u> in abundance, <u>have existence from non-existence</u>.
天下万物生于有,有生于无。

The Holy Bible

Let no man deceive you by any means: for that day shall not come, except there come a falling away first, and that man of sin be revealed, <u>the son of perdition</u>;

Who opposeth and exalteth himself above all that is called God, or that is worshipped; so that he as God sitteth in the temple of God, shewing himself that he is God.
2 Thessalonians 2:2-3

Who is the liar? It is whoever denies that Jesus is the Christ. Such a person is the antichrist--denying the Father and the Son.
1 John 2:22

<u>All things were made by him</u>; and without him was not any thing made that was made.
John 1:3

By faith we understand that the universe was formed at God's command, so that what is seen was <u>not made out of what was visible</u>.
Hebrews 11:3

The Tao Te Ching - Chapter 41

Superior scholar **hear the Way, diligent and go him**.
上士聞道，勤而行之。

Middle scholar hear the Way, seem exist as if dead.
中士聞道，若存若亡。

Inferior scholar hear the Way, big smile him.
下士聞道，大笑之。

No smile, not enough consider take part in the Way.
不笑，不足以為道。

Hence, establish talk to have him. 故，建言有之。

Understand the Way seem dark. 明道若昧。

Enter the Way like retreating. 進道若退。

Barbarian the Way seem wicked. 夷道若纇。

Superior virtue like valley. 上德若谷。

Great pure seem disgrace. 大白若辱。

Vast virtue seem not enough. 广德若不足。

Build virtue like thief. 建德若偷。

Substance true like change. 質真若渝。

Big square without corner. 大方无隅。

Big instrument late win. 大器晚成。

Big sound rare voice. 大音希声。

Big image without form. 大象无形。

The Way hidden, <u>not have name</u>. 道隱，无名。

Man only the Way, perfect **pardon** and accomplish.
夫唯道，善貸且成。

The Holy Bible

My sheep <u>hear My voice</u>, and I know them, <u>and they follow Me</u>;
John 10:27

The same day went Jesus out of the house, and sat by the sea side.

And great multitudes were gathered together unto him, so that he went into a ship, and sat; and the whole multitude stood on the shore.

And he spake many things unto them in parables, saying, Behold, a sower went forth to sow;

And when he sowed, some seeds fell by the way side, and the fowls came and devoured them up:

Some fell upon stony places, where they had not much earth: and forthwith they sprung up, because they had no deepness of earth:

And when the sun was up, they were scorched; and because they had no root, they withered away.

And some fell among thorns; and the thorns sprung up, and choked them:

But other fell into good ground, and brought forth fruit, some an hundredfold, some sixtyfold, some thirtyfold.

<u>Who hath ears to hear, let him hear</u>.   Matthew 13:1-9

Then came Peter to him, and said, <u>Lord</u>, how oft shall my brother sin against me, <u>and I **forgive** him</u>? till seven times? Jesus saith unto him, I say not unto thee, Until seven times: but, Until seventy times seven.   Matthew 18:21-22

The Tao Te Ching - Chapter 42

The Way give birth to one. 道生一。
One give birth to two. 一生二。
Two give birth to three. 二生三。
<u>Three</u> give birth to ten thousand things. 三生万物。

<u>Ten thousand things carry yin, and hold in arms, yang</u>.
万物負阴，而抱，阳。

Opposition spirit believe change peaceful. 冲气以為和。

People him place hate, exclusively become <u>orphaned</u>, <u>widowed</u>, <u>no grain</u>, yet <u>King</u> just to serve as name.
人之所惡，唯孤，寡，不谷，而王公以為稱。

Therefore, matter perhaps to harm him yet benefit.
故，物或損之而益。

Perhaps increase him, as well as damage. 或益之，而損。

People him place teaching, I also <u>teach</u>. Him strong bridge person. No get his death.
人之所教，我亦教。 之強梁者。 不得其死。

<u>I use belief called, teach Father</u>. 吾将以為，教父。

The Holy Bible

And Jesus came and spoke to them, saying, "All authority has been given to Me in heaven and on earth. Go therefore and make disciples of all the nations, baptizing them in the name of <u>the Father and of the Son and of the Holy Spirit</u>, teaching them to observe all things that I have commanded you; and lo, I am with you always, even to the end of the age." Amen.
Matthew 28:18-20

I am astonished that you are so quickly deserting the one who called you to live in the grace of Christ and are <u>turning to a different gospel-- which is really no gospel at all</u>.

Evidently some people are throwing you into confusion and are trying to pervert the gospel of Christ. But even if we or an angel from heaven should preach a gospel other than the one we preached to you, let them be under God's curse!
Galatians 1:6-8

The thief comes only to <u>steal</u> and <u>kill</u> and <u>destroy</u>; I have come that they may have life, and have it to the full.   John 10:10

On his robe and on his thigh he has this name written: <u>king of kings</u> and lord of lords.   Revelation 19:16

Then we will no longer be infants, tossed back and forth by the waves, and blown here and there by every wind of <u>teaching</u> and by the cunning and craftiness of people in their deceitful scheming.   Ephesians 4:14

Evildoers foster <u>rebellion against God</u>; the messenger of death will be sent against them.   Proverbs 17:11

The Tao Te Ching - Chapter 43

All under heaven him extremely flexible, speed hasten, all under heaven him extremely <u>strong</u>.
天下之至柔，馳騁，天下之至堅。

<u>Nothing exist to enter without opening</u>, I regard that understanding without change, him possess benefit.
无有入无间，吾是以知无為，之有益。

<u>No word him teaching, not become him increase</u>.
不言之教，无之益。

All under heaven <u>hope</u> reach him. 天下希及之。

The Holy Bible

And the great dragon was cast out, that old serpent, called the Devil, and Satan, which deceiveth the whole world: he was cast out into the earth, and his angels were cast out with him.

And I heard a loud voice saying in heaven, Now is come salvation, and <u>strength</u>, and the kingdom of our God, and the power of his Christ: for the accuser of our brethren is cast down, which accused them before our God day and night.
Revelation 12:9-10

Above all else, <u>guard your heart</u>, for everything you do flows from it. Proverbs 4:23

Jesus answered, "It is written: 'Man shall not live on bread alone, but <u>on every word that comes from the mouth of God</u>.'"
Matthew 4:4

May the God of hope fill you with all joy and peace as you trust in Him, so that you may overflow with <u>hope</u> by the power of the Holy Spirit. Romans 15:13

The Tao Te Ching - Chapter 44

Name together with person, who parent? 名与身,孰亲?

Person give goods, what more? 身与货,孰多?

Same as give death, which disease? 得与亡,孰病?

This reason very fond of necessary doctor expenses. 是故甚愛必大費。

Many hide most certainly substantial death. 多藏必厚亡。

Know enough not have abuse, understand detain to not endanger. 知足不辱。

Know only no danger. 知止不殆。

Can use to grow long time. 可以长久。

The Holy Bible

<u>The Son is the image of the invisible God</u>, the firstborn over all creation. <u>For in him all things were created</u>: things in heaven and on earth, visible and invisible, whether thrones or powers or rulers or authorities; all things have been created through him and for him. Colossians 1:15-16

Every <u>good gift</u> and every perfect gift is from above, and cometh down from the Father of lights, with whom is no variableness, neither shadow of turning. James 1:17

Praise the LORD, my soul, and forget not all his benefits-- who forgives all your sins and <u>heals all your diseases</u>, who redeems your life from the pit and crowns you with love and compassion, who satisfies your desires with good things so that your youth is renewed like the eagle's. Psalm 103:2-5

Just as <u>people are destined to die once</u>, and after that to face judgment, so Christ was sacrificed once to take away the sins of many; and he will appear a second time, not to bear sin, but to bring salvation to those who are waiting for him. Hebrews 9:27-28

And he causeth all, both small and great, rich and poor, free and bond, to receive a mark in their right hand, or in their foreheads: And that no man might buy or sell, <u>save he that had the mark</u>, or the name of the beast, or the number of his name. Revelation 13:16-17

But you, man of God, <u>f</u>lee from all this, and pursue righteousness, godliness, faith, love, endurance and gentleness. Fight the good fight of the faith. <u>Take hold of the eternal life</u> to which you were called when you made your good confession in the presence of many witnesses. 1 Timothy 6:11-12

The Tao Te Ching - Chapter 45

Great accomplish seem lack, his use not fraud.
大成若缺，其用不弊。

Great full seem to rush, his use not <u>exhausted</u>.
大盈若冲，其用不窮。

Great straight, <u>seem wronged</u>. 大直，若屈。

Great clever, seem clumsy. 大巧，若拙。

Great Word, <u>seem slow of speech</u>. 大辯，若訥。

Calm victorious impatient, <u>tremble victory heat</u>.
静胜躁，寒胜熱。

<u>Pure quiet</u> because all under heaven normal.
清静為天下正。

The Holy Bible

Do not be deceived: God cannot be mocked. A man reaps what he sows. Galatians 6:7

He will not allow your foot to slip; He who keeps you will not slumber. Behold, He who keeps Israel Will neither <u>slumber nor sleep</u>. Psalm 121:3-4

"Why? What crime has he committed?" asked Pilate. But they shouted all the louder, "<u>Crucify him</u>!" Matthew 27:23

The Lord is <u>not slow</u> about His promise, as some count slowness, but is patient toward you, not wishing for any to perish but for all to come to repentance. 2 Peter 3:9

And the sea gave up the dead which were in it, and death and Hades gave up the dead which were in them; and they were judged, every one of them according to their deeds. Then death and Hades were thrown into the <u>lake of fire</u>. This is the second death, the lake of fire. And if anyone's name was not found written in the book of life, he was thrown into the lake of fire. Revelation 20:14-15

The <u>wolf will live with the lamb</u>, the leopard will lie down with the goat, the calf and the lion and the yearling together; and a little child will lead them. Isaiah 11:6

The Tao Te Ching - Chapter 46

All under heaven have the Way, **retreat run horse** in manure.
天下有道，却走马以粪。

All under heaven without the way, **military horse living in suburbs**. 天下无道，戎马生于郊。

Disaster is not large, compared to not know satisfy.
祸莫大，于不知足。

Mistake is not large, compared to desire satisfied.
咎莫大，于欲得祸。

Hence, control satisfy him enough. Frequently satisfy!
故，知足之足常。足矣！

The Holy Bible

Now therefore, O kings, be wise;

be warned, O rulers of the earth.

Serve the Lord with fear,

and rejoice with trembling.

Kiss the Son,

lest he be angry, and you perish in the way,

for his wrath is quickly kindled.

Blessed are all who take refuge in him.

Psalm 2:10-12

The Tao Te Ching - Chapter 47

<u>Not go out door</u>, know all under heaven. 不出户，知天下。

Not spy <u>window</u>, see heaven The Way. 不闚牖，见天道。

His go out more distant, his <u>knowledge more inadequate</u>.
其出弥遠，其知弥少。

This use <u>sage</u> man not advance and understand. Not see, yet name. Not change, yet accomplish.
是以圣人不行而知。 不见，而明。 不為，而成。

The Holy Bible

I am the <u>door</u>: by me if any man enter in, he shall be saved, and <u>shall go in and out</u>, and find pasture.   John 10:9

Bring ye all the tithes into the storehouse, that there may be meat in mine house, and prove me now herewith, saith the LORD of hosts, if I will not open you the <u>windows of heaven</u>, and pour you out a blessing, that there shall not be room enough to receive it.   Malachi 3:10

The heart of the discerning <u>acquires knowledge</u>, for the ears of the wise seek it out.   Proverbs 18:15

The <u>wise</u> prevail through great power, and those who have knowledge muster their strength.   Proverbs 24:5

The Tao Te Ching - Chapter 48

Do <u>study</u> daily, increase. 為学日，益。

Do the Way daily, decrease. 為道日，損。

Decrease him again decrease, use until from nothing do. 損之又損，以至于无為。

<u>Nothing do and not do</u>. 无為而不為。

Take all under heaven, constant use without work, and **<u>him have work</u>**, not satisfy reason take all under heaven. 取天下，常以无事，及其有事，不足以取天下。

The Holy Bible

<u>Study</u> to shew thyself approved unto God, a workman that needeth not to be ashamed, rightly dividing the word of truth. But **shun profane and vain babblings**: for they will increase unto more ungodliness. 2 Timothy 2:16

For the wisdom of this world is foolishness with God. For it is written, <u>He taketh the wise in their own craftiness</u>. And again, The Lord knoweth the thoughts of the wise, that they are vain. Therefore let no man glory in men. For all things are yours; 1 Corinthians 3:19-21

As for you, you were dead in your transgressions and sins, in which you used to live when you followed the ways of this world and of the ruler of the kingdom of the air, **the spirit** <u>who is now at work</u> in those who are disobedient. Ephesians 2:1-2

The Tao Te Ching - Chapter 49

Sage person without normal mind. <u>Use ordinary people mind</u>, serve as mind. 圣人无常心。以百姓心，為心。

Good person, I like him. 善者，吾善之。

<u>Not good person, I also good, him character good.</u>
不善者，吾亦善之德善。

True person, <u>I believe him</u>. 信者，吾信之。

<u>Not true person, I also believe him, character true.</u>
不信者，吾亦信之，德信。

Sage people exist all under heaven, named name how?
圣人在天下，歙歙焉？

Reason all under heaven **muddy his intention**.
為天下渾其心。

Many people all focus their ears eyes sage man, all <u>children his</u>. 百姓皆注其耳目圣人，皆孩之。

The Holy Bible

Be sober-minded; be watchful. Your adversary the devil prowls around like a roaring lion, <u>seeking someone to devour</u>.
1 Peter 5:8

<u>Woe to those who call evil good and good evil</u>, who put darkness for light and light for darkness, who put bitter for sweet and sweet for bitter.
Isaiah 5:20

And you were dead in the trespasses and sins in which you once walked, following the course of this world, <u>following the prince of the power of the air</u>, the spirit that is now at work in the sons of disobedience.
Ephesians 2:1-2

<u>A righteous person who yields to the wicked is like **a muddied spring**</u> or a polluted well.
Proverbs 25:26

For ye are all the children of God by faith in Christ Jesus.
Galatians 3:26

Even <u>a child is known by his doings</u>, whether his work be pure, and whether it be right.
Proverbs 20:11

The Tao Te Ching - Chapter 50

<u>Give birth life, enter death</u>. 出生入死。

Life him follower, ten have three. 生之徒，十有三。

Death him follower, ten have three. 死之徒，十有三。

<u>People him **life to change**</u>, him regard impassable place, also ten have three. 人之生，动之于死地，亦十有三。

Man what happening? 夫何故？

Because of His Life, life him thick. 以其生，生之厚。

<u>Hide news good</u>, absorb living person. 盖聞善，攝生者。

Land travel not encounter fierce tiger, enter army not to meet with first soldiers. 陸行不遇凶虎，入軍不被甲兵。

Murder without place to drop his horn. 凶无所投其角。

Tiger without place to use his claws. 虎无所用其爪。

Private without place to hold his sword. 兵无所容其刃。

Man what happening? 夫何故？

According to his no death earth. 以其无死地。

The Holy Bible

Surely <u>I was sinful at birth</u>, sinful from the time my mother conceived me.   Psalm 51:5

Jesus replied, "Very truly I tell you, no one can see the kingdom of God <u>unless they are **born again**</u>."   John 3:3

Therefore if anyone is in Christ, **he is a new creature**; the old things passed away; behold, new things have come.   2 Corinthians 5:17

Summoning the crowd along with His disciples, He said to them, "If anyone wants to be My follower, he must deny himself, take up his cross, and follow Me. For whoever wants to save his life will lose it, but whoever loses his life because of Me and **the gospel** will save it.

For what does it benefit a man to gain the whole world yet lose his life? What can a man give in exchange for his life? For whoever is ashamed of Me and of My words in this adulterous and sinful generation, the Son of Man will also be ashamed of him when He comes in the glory of His Father with the holy angels."   Mark 8:34-36

Indeed, all who desire to live godly in Christ Jesus will be persecuted. **But evil men and impostors will proceed from bad to worse, deceiving and being deceived**. You, however, continue in the things you have learned and become convinced of, knowing from whom you have learned them, and that from childhood you have known the sacred writings which are able to give you the wisdom that leads to salvation through faith which is in Christ Jesus.   2 Timothy 3:12-15

The Tao Te Ching - Chapter 51

The Way give birth to him, virtue raised him.
道生之，德畜之。

<u>Matter formed him</u>, conditions complete him.
物形之，势成之。

This because ten thousand thing, nothing not respect the Way and noble virtue. 是以万物，莫不尊道而貴德。

The Way him honor, morality him valuable, <u>man is not him, life same as common,</u> oneself true.
道之尊，德之貴，夫莫之，命而常，自然。

Hence, the Way to grow him virtue, to raise him, always him nourish him pavilion. Him poison him.
故，道生之德，畜之，长之育之亭。之毒之。

Raise him, cover him. 養之，覆之。

Give birth to yet, not exist. 生而，不有。

Serve as, but not rely on. 為，而不恃。

Grow and not slaughter. 长而不宰。

That called <u>profound virtue</u>. 是謂玄德。

The Holy Bible

Then God said, "Let us make mankind in our image, in our likeness, so that they may rule over the fish in the sea and the birds in the sky, over the livestock and all the wild animals, and over all the creatures that move along the ground." Genesis 1:26

Then <u>the LORD God formed a man</u> from the dust of the ground and breathed into his nostrils the breath of life, and the man became a living being. Genesis 2:7

God created man in His own image, in the image of God He created him; male and female He created them. Genesis 1:27

His divine power has given us <u>everything we need for a godly life through our knowledge of him who called us **by his own glory**</u> and goodness. Through these he has given us his very great and precious promises, so that **through them you may participate in the divine nature**, having escaped the corruption in the world caused by evil desires.

For this very reason, make every effort to add to your faith goodness; and to goodness, knowledge; and to knowledge, self-control; and to self-control, perseverance; and to perseverance, godliness; and to godliness, mutual affection; and to mutual affection, love. 2 Peter 1:3-7

Now these three remain: faith, hope, and love. But <u>the greatest of these is love</u>. 1 Corinthians 13:13

The Tao Te Ching - Chapter 52

All under heaven have <u>beginning</u>, believe create all <u>under heaven mother</u>. 天下有始，以為天下母。

Then need <u>his mother</u>, use to know her son.
既得其母，以知其子。

Already know her son, again guard his mother.
既知其子，复守其母。

End life not dangerous. 没身不殆。

Stop his exchange, <u>shut his gate</u>, <u>end life not diligent</u>.
塞其兌，閉其門，終身不勤。

Open his exchange, aid their affairs, end life not <u>saved</u>.
開其兌，济其事，終身不救。

See his young called bright, observe gentle called powerful.
见其小曰明，守柔曰强。

Use his light, recover to return him to understand, without losing life calamity. 用其光，复归其明，无遗身殃。

This means to <u>study</u> always. 是為習常。

The Holy Bible

In the **beginning was the Word**, and the Word was with God, and the Word was God.   John 1:1

Salvation is found in no one else, for there is <u>no other name under heaven</u> given to mankind by which we must be saved.   Acts 4:12

This is how the birth of Jesus the Messiah came about: <u>His mother Mary</u> was pledged to be married to Joseph, but before they came together, she was found to be pregnant through the Holy Spirit.   Matthew 1:18

That which was from the beginning, which we have heard, which we have seen with our eyes, which we have looked at and our hands have touched--this we proclaim concerning the **Word of life**.   1 John 1:1

Enter through the narrow gate. For wide is the gate and broad is the road that leads to destruction, and many enter through it. But <u>small is the gate and narrow the road that leads to life, and only a few find it</u>.   Matthew 7:13-14

For whosoever shall call upon the name of the Lord <u>shall be saved</u>.

How then shall they call on him in whom they have not believed? and how shall they believe in him of whom they have not heard? and how shall they hear without a preacher?   Romans 10:13-14

<u>Study</u> to shew thyself approved unto God, a workman that needeth not to be ashamed, rightly dividing the word of truth.   2 Timothy 2:15

The Tao Te Ching - Chapter 53

Cause me to lie between true person knowledge. Travel in great Way, <u>only distribute that fear</u>.
使我介然有知。 行于大道，唯施是畏。

Great Way very barbarian and man be fond of path.
大道甚夷而人好徑。

Government very divided, field very over grown with weeds, <u>storehouse very empty</u>.
朝甚除，田甚芜，倉甚虛。

Clothes formal color, **carry sharp sword, satiate drink, eat, money, goods only remainder.**
服文彩，帶利劍，厭飲，食，財，貨有余。

That called **steal to boast**. Wrong Way also!
是謂盜夸。 非道也哉！

The Holy Bible

So then, my beloved, just as you have always obeyed, not as in my presence only, but now much more in my absence, <u>work out your salvation with fear and trembling</u>; for it is God who is at work in you, both to will and to work for His good pleasure.
Philippians 2:12-13

By smooth talk and flattery they deceive the minds of naive people.   Romans 16:18

Then He continued by saying to them, "Nation will rise against nation and kingdom against kingdom, and there will be great earthquakes, and in various places plagues and <u>famines</u>; and there will be terrors and great signs from heaven.
Luke 21:11

And that no man might buy or sell, save he that had the mark, or **the name of the beast**, or the number of his name.
Revelation 13:17

And they worshipped the dragon which gave power unto the beast: and **they worshipped the beast**, saying, Who is like unto the beast? who is able to make war with him?   Revelation 13:4

I am the LORD; that is my name! **I will not yield my glory to another** or my praise to idols.   Isaiah 42:8

The Tao Te Ching - Chapter 54

Good establish not uproot. Good hold in arms person not escape. 善建者不拔。 善抱者不脫。

Children grandchildren to use offering, sacrifice not stop. 子孫以祭，祀不輟。

Cultivate him in regard to life, that character to be true. 修之于身，其德乃真。

Cultivate him in regard to family, their good deeds only remainder. 修之于家，其德乃余。

Cultivate him in regard to village, such morality therefore to develop. 修之于鄉，其德乃长。

Cultivate him in regard to nation, its morality therefore to be abundant. 修之于邦，其德乃丰。

Cultivate him in regard to all under heaven, his morality to be universal. 修之于天下，其德乃普。

Happening because person to <u>observe life</u>. 故以身觀身。

<u>Use family to watch family</u>. 以家觀家。

Use village to watch village. 以鄉觀鄉。

Use nation to watch nation. 以邦觀邦。

Use all under heaven to watch all under heaven. 以天下觀天下。

<u>We who use knowledge</u> all under heaven correct! 吾何以知天下然哉！

<u>Use this</u>. 以此。

The Holy Bible

His divine power has granted to us all things that pertain to life and godliness, through the knowledge of him who called us to his own glory and excellence, by which he has granted to us his precious and very great promises, so that through them you may become partakers of the divine nature, having escaped from the corruption that is in the world because of sinful desire.

For this very reason, make every effort to supplement your faith with virtue, and virtue with knowledge, and knowledge with self-control, and self-control with steadfastness, and steadfastness with godliness, and godliness with brotherly affection, and brotherly affection with love. For if these qualities are yours and are increasing, they keep you from being ineffective or unfruitful in the knowledge of our Lord Jesus Christ.   2 Peter 1:3-8

And they overcame him by the blood of the Lamb, and by the word of their testimony; <u>and they loved not their lives unto the death</u>.
Revelation 12:11

If the world hate you, ye know that it hated me before it hated you.
John 15:18

<u>Brother will betray brother to death</u>, and a father his child; children will rebel against their parents and have them put to death. You will be hated by everyone because of me, but the one who stands firm to the end will be saved.   Matthew 10:21-22

Truly, truly, I say to you, <u>we speak of what we know</u> and testify of what we have seen, and you do not accept our testimony.
John 3:11

Teaching them to <u>observe everything I have commanded you</u>. And remember, I am with you always, to the end of the age.
Matthew 28:19

The Tao Te Ching - Chapter 55

Contain kindness him generous, compare to red son.
含德之厚，比于赤子。

Poison <u>insect</u> no sting, violent beast not seize, seize bird not strike. 毒虫不螫，猛獸不据，攫鸟不搏。

<u>Bone weak, muscle soft</u>, yet grasp strong.
骨弱，筋柔，而握固。

Have not known female, male her to join, this complete to make. 未知牝，牡之合，而全作。

Energy him arrive, too. 精之至，也。

End sun, cry and not hoarse voice. 終日，号而不嗄。

Mix together, him arrive also to know union called constant. 和，之至也知和曰常。

Know constant called bright. 知常曰明。

<u>Benefit life called good</u>. 益生曰祥。

<u>Mind use spirit called powerful</u>. 心使气曰强。

Matter to strengthen rule old called, <u>him not the Way</u>. 物壮則老謂，之不道。

<u>Not the Way soon end</u>. 不道早已。

The Holy Bible

Whoever believes in the Son has eternal life, but whoever rejects the Son will not see life, for God's wrath remains on them.
John 3:36

All flying <u>insects</u> are unclean to you; do not eat them.
Leviticus 11:20

For our struggle is not against <u>flesh and blood</u>, but against the rulers, against the authorities, against the powers of this dark world and against the spiritual forces of evil in the heavenly realms.
Ephesians 6:12

Listen to my instruction and be wise; do not disregard it. Blessed are those who listen to me, watching daily at my doors, waiting at my doorway.

For those who <u>find me find life</u> and receive favor from the LORD. But those who fail to find me harm themselves; all who hate me love death.
Proverbs 8:33-36

The mind governed by the flesh is death, but the <u>mind governed by the Spirit is life and peace</u>.
Romans 8:6

"I am the Alpha and the Omega," says the Lord God, "<u>who is</u>, and who was, <u>and who is to come</u>, the Almighty."
Revelation 1:8

The Tao Te Ching - Chapter 56

<u>Know,</u> person not talk, talk, person not know.
知，者不言，言，者不知。

Subdue their sharp, <u>divide their confused</u>. 挫其銳，解其紛。

<u>Blend their light together with his dirt</u>. 和其光同其尘。

This is called dark similar. 是謂玄同。

Reason not able obtain, yet closely related.
故不可得，而亲。

Not able to permit, yet sparse. 不可得，而疏。

Not able to obtain, but beneficial. 不可得，而利。

Not able to have and evil. 不可得而害。

Not able to obtain, yet expensive. 不可得，而貴。

Not able to obtain, yet inexpensive. 不可得，而賤。

Hence, serve as all under heaven <u>expensive</u>. 故，為天下貴。

The Holy Bible

If anyone supposes that he <u>knows</u> anything, he has not yet known as he ought to know; but if anyone loves God, he is known by Him.
1 Corinthians 8:3

All the nations will be gathered before him, and <u>he will separate the people</u> one from another as a shepherd separates the sheep from the goats.

He will put the sheep on his right and the goats on his left. Then the King will say to those on his right, 'Come, you who are blessed by my Father; take your inheritance, the kingdom prepared for you since the creation of the world. Then he will say to those on his left, 'Depart from me, you who are cursed, into the eternal fire prepared for the devil and his angels.   Matthew 25:32-34; 41

And this is the condemnation, that light is come into the world, and <u>men loved darkness rather than light</u>, because their deeds were evil. For every one that doeth evil hateth the light, neither cometh to the light, lest his deeds should be reproved. But he that doeth truth cometh to the light, that his deeds may be made manifest, that they are wrought in God.   John 3:19-21

For the <u>wages</u> of sin is death, but the gift of God is eternal life in Christ Jesus our Lord.   Romans 6:23

The Tao Te Ching - Chapter 57

<u>Use correct rule country</u>, because strange to use soldiers.
以正治国，以奇用兵。

Use without work to obtain all under heaven.
以无事取天下。

We who use know that correct! According to this.
吾何以知其然哉！以此。

All under heaven many jealous, avoid mentioning, but the people completely impoverished.
天下多忌，諱，而民弥貧。

People many sharp instruments, country residence grow dark.
民多利器，国家滋昏。

Man much skill clever, strange thing weeping begin.
人多伎巧，奇物泫起。

Law decree increase manifest thief traitors exist.
法令滋彰盗賊多有。

Reason sage man say, I without do and the people self change.
故圣人云，我无為而民自化。

I good quiet and the people self correct.
我好静而民自正。

I without work and the people self rich.
我无事而民自富。

I without desire and the people self simple.
我无欲而民自朴。

The Holy Bible

The words of the wise heard in quietness are better than the shouting of a ruler among fools. <u>Wisdom is better than weapons of war, but one sinner destroys much good.</u>   Ecclesiastes 9:18

> Why do the nations rage
>
> and the peoples plot in vain?
>
> The kings of the earth set themselves,
>
> and the rulers take counsel together,
>
> against the Lord and against his Anointed, saying,
>
> "Let us burst their bonds apart
>
> and cast away their cords from us."
>
> He who sits in the heavens laughs;
>
> the Lord holds them in derision.
>
> Then he will speak to them in his wrath,
>
> and terrify them in his fury, saying,
>
> "As for me, I have set my King
>
> on Zion, my holy hill."

Psalm 2:1-6

The Tao Te Ching - Chapter 58

His government depressed gloomy, his people simple honest.
其政悶悶，其民淳淳。

His government investigate examine, his people lack scarce.
其政察察，其民缺缺。

Disaster still good fortune him actually rely upon.
禍尚福之所倚。

Good fortune still disaster him actually conceal.
福尚禍之所伏。

Who know his extreme? His without principle.
孰知其極？其无正。

Upstanding repeatedly serve as strange, good again serve as evil. 正复為奇，善复為妖。

Man him confuse, his sun solid long time.
人之迷，其日固久。

This use sage man square, but not cut. 是以圣人方，而不割。

Inexpensive, but not cut off. 廉，而不劌。

Straight, yet not store. 直，而不肆。

Light, but not brilliant. 光，而不耀。

The Holy Bible

He will cause deceit to prosper, and he will consider himself superior. When they feel secure, he will destroy many and take his stand against the Prince of princes. Yet he will be destroyed, but not by human power.   Daniel 8:25

His mouth is full of cursing and deceit and fraud: under his tongue is mischief and vanity.

He sitteth in the lurking places of the villages: in the secret places doth he murder the innocent: his eyes are privily set against the poor.

He lieth in wait secretly as a lion in his den: he lieth in wait to catch the poor: he doth catch the poor, when he draweth him into his net.

He croucheth, and humbleth himself, that the poor may fall by his strong ones.

He hath said in his heart, God hath forgotten: he hideth his face; he will never see it.

Arise, O LORD; O God, lift up thine hand: forget not the humble.

Why does the wicked man revile God? Why does he say to himself, "He won't call me to account"?

But you, God, see the trouble of the afflicted; you consider their grief and take it in hand. The victims commit themselves to you; you are the helper of the fatherless.

Break the arm of the wicked and the evildoer, Seek out his wickedness until You find none.

The LORD is King for ever and ever: the heathen are perished out of his land.   Psalm 10:7-16

The Tao Te Ching - Chapter 59

Govern persons work, heaven do not seem sparing.
治人事，天莫若嗇。

Man only sparing, this called early submission.
夫唯嗇，是謂早服。

Early submission called him repeat accumulate virtue.
早服謂之重積德。

Repeat accumulate virtue, <u>nothing can not overcome</u>.
重積德，則无不克。

Nothing can not overcome, then none who know his utmost.
无不克，則莫知其极。

Do not know his utmost, can use occupy country.
莫知其极，可以有国。

Occupy country him mother, can use to grow long time.
有国之母，可以长久。

This called deep root solid <u>foundation</u>. Long life observe him the Way. 是謂深根固柢。 长生久视之道。

The Holy Bible

Everyone who believes that Jesus is the Christ has been born of God, and everyone who loves the Father loves whoever has been born of him.

By this we know that we love the children of God, when we love God and obey his commandments. For this is the love of God, that we keep his commandments. And his commandments are not burdensome.

<u>For everyone who has been born of God overcomes the world</u>. And this is the victory that has overcome the world—our faith.
1 John 5:1-4

According to the grace of God which was given to me, like a wise master builder I laid a <u>foundation</u>, and another is building on it. But each man must be careful how he builds on it.

For no man can lay a foundation other than the one which is laid, which is Jesus Christ.

Now if any man builds on the foundation with gold, silver, precious stones, wood, hay, straw their work will be shown for what it is, because the Day will bring it to light. It will be revealed with fire, and the fire will test the quality of each person's work. If what has been built survives, the builder will receive a reward. If it is burned up, the builder will suffer loss but yet will be saved--even though only as one escaping through the flames.
1 Corinthians 3:10-15

The Tao Te Ching - Chapter 60

Govern big country like cooking small fresh fish.
治大国若烹小鲜。

Use the Way manage all under heaven. 以道莅天下。

His ghost not spirit. 其鬼不神。

Wrong, his ghost not God. 非，其鬼不神。

His spirit <u>not wound people</u>. 其神不傷人。

Wrong, his mind not injure man. 非，其神不傷人。

Sage man also not wound man. 圣人亦不傷人。

Man both not each other wound, cause morality mix return.
夫兩不相傷，故德交归焉。

The Holy Bible

As Jesus was walking beside the Sea of Galilee, he saw two brothers, Simon called Peter and his brother Andrew. They were casting a net into the lake, for they were fishermen.

And He said to them, "Follow Me, and I will make you fishers of men." At once they left their nets and followed him.

Going on from there, he saw two other brothers, James son of Zebedee and his brother John. They were in a boat with their father Zebedee, preparing their nets. Jesus called them, and immediately they left the boat and their father and followed him.

Jesus went throughout Galilee, teaching in their synagogues, proclaiming the good news of the kingdom, <u>and healing every disease and sickness among the people</u>.

News about him spread all over Syria, and people brought to him all who were ill with various diseases, those suffering severe pain, the demon-possessed, those having seizures, and the paralyzed; and he healed them.

Large crowds from Galilee, the Decapolis, Jerusalem, Judea and the region across the Jordan followed him.

Matthew 4:18-25

The Tao Te Ching - Chapter 61

Big country person decline to spread, all under heaven him deliver. 大国者下流，天下之交。

<u>All under heaven him gorge</u>. 天下之牝。

<u>Female often use quiet victory</u>, male often use <u>calm</u> become inferior. 牝常以静胜，牡以静為下。

Reason big country lead inferior small country, rule capture small country. 故大国以下小国，則取小国。

Small country use <u>inferior, great country rule</u> to get great country. 小国以下，大国則取大国。

Reason perhaps <u>inferior so as to take</u>, perhaps inferior, yet get. 故或下以取，或下，而取。

Big country not pass by desire, combine animals people. 大国不过欲，兼畜人。

Small country not pass by desire, enter affair person. 小国不过欲，入事人。

Man both person each allow place desire. 夫兩者各得所欲。

Great person should act as inferior. 大者宜為下。

The Holy Bible

If the world hates you, keep in mind that <u>it hated me first</u>. If you belonged to the world, it would love you as its own. As it is, you do not belong to the world, but I have chosen you out of the world. That is why the world hates you. Remember what I told you: 'A servant is not greater than his master.' If they persecuted me, they will persecute you also. If they obeyed my teaching, they will obey yours also. They will treat you this way because of my name, for they do not know the one who sent me. If I had not come and spoken to them, they would not be guilty of sin; but now they have no excuse for their sin.   John 15:18-21

The <u>quiet words of the wise</u> are more to be heeded than the shouts of a ruler of fools.   Ecclesiastes 9:17

The one who has knowledge uses words with restraint, and whoever has understanding is <u>even-tempered</u>. Even fools are thought wise if they keep silent, and discerning if they hold their tongues.   Proverbs 17:27-28

Blessed are the <u>meek, for they will inherit the earth</u>.   Matthew 5:5

But <u>the saints of the most High shall take the kingdom</u>, and possess the kingdom for ever, even for ever and ever.   Daniel 7:18

You have made them to be a kingdom and priests to our God; and **they will reign** upon the earth.   Revelation 5:10

Blessed and holy are those who share in the first resurrection. The second death has no power over them, but **they will be priests of God and of Christ and will reign with Him for a thousand years**.   Revelation 20:6

It is a trustworthy statement: For if we died with Him, we will also live with Him; **If we endure, we will also reign with Him**; If we deny Him, He also will deny us; If we are faithless, He remains faithful, for He cannot deny Himself.   2 Timothy 2:12

The Tao Te Ching - Chapter 62

The Way person ten thousand things him <u>mysterious</u>.
道者万物之奥。

Good man him treasure, not good him to defend.
善人之宝，不善人之所保。

<u>Beautiful words can use market honor</u>. 美言可以市尊。

<u>Beautiful behavior can increase man</u>. 美行可以加人。

Man him not good, why throw away him exist?
人之不善，何弃之有？

Reason set up Heaven Son, establish three honorable.
故立天子，置三公。

Only retain bow jade with hole. 虽有拱璧。

Command first team of <u>four horses</u>. 以先驷马。

Not sit to advance these, this the Way. 不如坐進，此道。

Age-old him place so noble the Way, why?
古之所以貴此道，者何。

Not say: beg in order to obtain. <u>Have crime</u>. Use excuse evil?
不曰：求以得。有罪。以免邪？

Hence, act as all under heaven expensive.
故爲天下貴。

The Holy Bible

And he said to the human race, "The fear of the Lord--that is wisdom, and <u>to shun evil is understanding</u>."   Job 28:28

They worshiped the dragon because he gave his authority to the beast; and they worshiped the beast, saying, "<u>Who is like the beast</u>, and who is able to wage war with him?"
      Revelation 13:4

<u>Beware of practicing your righteousness before other people</u> in order to be seen by them, for then you will have no reward from your Father who is in heaven.   Matthew 6:1

I looked, and there before me was <u>a **white** horse</u>! Its rider held a bow, and he was given a crown, and he rode out as a conqueror bent on conquest.   Revelation 6:2

Then another horse came out, <u>a **fiery red** one</u>.

When the Lamb opened the third seal, I heard the third living creature say, "Come!" I looked, and there before me was <u>a **black** horse</u>! Its rider was holding a pair of scales in his hand.   Revelation 6:4-5

I looked, and there before me was <u>a **pale** horse</u>! Its rider was named Death, and Hades was following close behind him.   Revelation 6:8

But each one is tempted when he is carried away and enticed by his own lust. Then when lust has conceived, it gives birth to sin; and <u>when sin is accomplished, it brings forth death</u>.   James 1:14-15

The Tao Te Ching - Chapter 63

Do <u>without do</u>. 為无為。

Work without work. 事无事。

Smell without smell. 味无味。

Large small, many few, <u>report blame</u> according to goodness. 大小，多少，报怨以德。

<u>Plan difficulty in regard to their easy</u>. 圖難于其易。

Act as great in regard to their fine. 為大于其細。

All under heaven difficult thing, certainly to take in change. 天下難事，必作于易。

All under heaven large matter, certainly to take in regard to fine. 天下大事，必作于細。

This according to sage man, <u>death not become great</u>. 是以圣人，終不為大。

<u>Reason</u> can become their great. 故能成其大。

<u>Man light promise will few believe</u>. 夫輕諾必寡信。

Much easy will many scold. 多易必多難。

That because of sage man still difficult. <u>Him reason death without scold</u>! 是以圣人難犹。 之故終无難矣!

The Holy Bible

"I am the vine; you are the branches. If you remain in me and I in you, you will bear much fruit; <u>apart from me you can do nothing</u>". John 15:5

<u>Then shall they deliver you up to be afflicted, and shall kill you</u>: and ye shall be hated of all nations for my name's sake. And then shall many be offended, and shall betray one another, and shall hate one another. And many false prophets shall rise, and shall deceive many. And because iniquity shall abound, the love of many shall wax cold. <u>But he that shall endure unto the end, the same shall be saved</u>. And this gospel of the kingdom shall be preached in all the world for a witness unto all nations; and then shall the end come. Matthew 24:9-14

And the third angel followed them, saying with a loud voice, If any man worship the beast and his image, and receive his mark in his forehead, or in his hand, <u>The same shall drink of the wine of the wrath of God</u>, which is poured out without mixture into the cup of his indignation; and he shall be tormented with fire and brimstone in the presence of the holy angels, and in the presence of the Lamb: Revelation 14:8-10

Come now, and let us <u>reason</u> together, saith the LORD: though your sins be as scarlet, they shall be as white as snow; though they be red like crimson, they shall be as wool. Isaiah 1:18

The LORD said to him, "<u>Who gave human beings their mouths</u>? Who makes them deaf or mute? Who gives them sight or makes them blind? Is it not I, the LORD? Exodus 4:11

The sting of death is sin, and the power of sin is the law. But thanks be to God! <u>He gives us the victory through our Lord Jesus Christ</u>. 1 Corinthians 15:56-57

The Tao Te Ching - Chapter 64

Their steady change hold. Their <u>not yet omen</u>, easy scheme.
其安易持。 其未兆,易謀。
Their brittle easy disperse, their tiny easy scatter.
其脆易泮,其微易散。
Act as him exist not yet occupy, execute these using not yet revolt. 為之于未有,治之于未乱。
Unite embrace him **tree of life**, with long end.
合抱之木生,于毫末。

<u>Nine stratum him platform</u>, begin from tired earth.
九層之台起于累土。
Thousand year him travel, start by foot down.
千里之行始于足下。

Because person decline him, <u>execute person</u> neglect him.
為者敗之,执者失之。
That according to sage man, nothing do, reason nothing be defeated. 是以圣人,无為,故无敗。
Nothing execute reason nothing to lose. 无执故无失。

People him cause to follow always in regard to how much win and defeat him. 民之从事常于几,成而敗之。
Careful end such as beginning, follow without be defeated work. 慎終如始,則无敗事。

That according to sage man. Desire not desire, not precious difficult to obtain him goods.
是以圣人。 欲不欲, 不貴難得之貨。
Study not learn, duplicate masses people him place cross.
学不学,复众人之所过。
Use to compliment ten thousand thing. Himself correct, yet not dare to be. 以輔万物。 之自然,而不敢為。

The Holy Bible

Above all, you must understand that in the last days scoffers will come, scoffing and following their own evil desires. They will say, "<u>Where is this 'coming' he promised?</u> Ever since our ancestors died, everything goes on as it has since the beginning of creation."
2 Peter 3:3-4

Blessed are they that do his commandments, that they may have right to the **tree of life**, and may enter in through the gates into the city.
Revelation 22:14

And he laid hold on the dragon, that old serpent, which is the Devil, and Satan, and bound him **a thousand years**, And cast him into the bottomless pit, and shut him up, and set a seal upon him, <u>that he should deceive the nations no more, till the thousand years should be fulfilled</u>: and after that he must be loosed a little season.
Revelation 20:2-3

Beloved, do not be surprised at the fiery trial when it comes upon you to test you, as though something strange were happening to you. But rejoice insofar as <u>you share Christ's sufferings</u>, that you may also rejoice and be glad when his glory is revealed. If you are insulted for the name of Christ, you are blessed, because the Spirit of glory and of God rests upon you.
1 Peter 4:12-14

For it is better, if it is God's will, to suffer for doing good than for doing evil.
1 Peter 3:17

"This, then, is how you should pray: "'Our Father in heaven, hallowed be your name, your kingdom come, your will be done, on earth as it is in heaven. Give us today our daily bread., and forgive us our debts, as we also have forgiven our debtors. And lead us not into temptation, but deliver us from the evil one. Amen.'
Matthew 6:9-13

The Tao Te Ching - Chapter 65

Ancient him good to become the Way person. <u>Not to use bright people</u>. 古之善為道者，非以明民。

Prepared according to <u>stupid him</u>. 将以愚之。
<u>**People it difficult to harness**</u>, use his wisdom much.
民之難治，以其智多。

Hence, use wisdom rule country, country him thief.
故，以智治国，国之賊。

No use wisdom to control country, country him good fortune.
不以智治国，国之福。

Know this, <u>**both person also bow to the ground type**</u>.
知此，兩者亦稽式。

Constant know bow to the ground type, <u>this called dark virtue</u>.
常知稽式，是謂玄德。

Dark virtue profound! Remote! <u>Give matter consideration</u>.
玄德深矣! 遠矣！与物反矣。

Thus, later in time, <u>you reach great obey</u>.
然后乃至大順。

The Holy Bible

<u>They are darkened in their understanding</u> and separated from the life of God because of the ignorance that is in them due to the hardening of their hearts. Ephesians 4:18

Then **<u>you will be handed over</u>** to be persecuted and put to death, and you will be hated by all nations <u>because of Me</u>. Matthew 24:9

And if it is evil in your eyes to serve the LORD, **<u>choose this day whom you will serve</u>**, whether the gods your fathers served in the region beyond the River, or the gods of the Amorites in whose land you dwell. But as for me and my house, we will serve the LORD." Joshua 24:15

<u>The way of the wicked is as darkness</u>: they know not at what they stumble. My son, attend to my words; incline thine ear unto my sayings. Let them not depart from thine eyes; keep them in the midst of thine heart. For they are life unto those that find them, and health to all their flesh.

Keep thy heart with all diligence; for out of it are the issues of life. Put away from thee a froward mouth, and perverse lips put far from thee. Let thine eyes look right on, and let thine eyelids look straight before thee. <u>Ponder the path of thy feet, and let all thy ways be established. Turn not to the right hand nor to the left: remove thy foot from evil</u>. Proverbs 4:19-27

He will oppose and will exalt himself over everything that is called God or is worshiped, so that <u>he sets himself up in God's temple</u>, proclaiming himself to be God. 2 Thessalonians 2:4

The Tao Te Ching - Chapter 66

<u>River sea</u>, these location have ability make numerous bewildered king people. 江海，之所以能為百谷王者。

Use their good inferior, him cause energy to become numerous valley king. 以其善下，之故能為百谷王。

That according to sage man. 是以圣人。

Desire superior people, must use talk down him.
欲上民，必以言下之。

Desire former people, must believe life after this.
欲先民，必以身后之。

That according to sage man. 是以圣人。

Live superior and people not heavy, live former and people not cause trouble. 处上而民不重，处前而民不害。

This use all under heaven instrument push and not reject.
是以天下樂推而不厭。

Use that not contend. 以其不争。

<u>Reason all under heaven, there is none capable take part in him fight</u>. 故天下，莫能与之争。

The Holy Bible

Then the angel showed me **the river** of the water of life, as clear as crystal, flowing from the throne of God and of the Lamb
Revelation 22:1

The dragon stood on the shore of the sea. And I saw a beast coming out of the sea. It had ten horns and seven heads, with ten crowns on its horns, and on each head a blasphemous name.
Revelation 13:1

The Tao Te Ching - Chapter 67

All under heaven everybody say <u>I the Way</u>. Great appearing, not resembling. 天下皆謂我道。 大似，不肖。

Man alone great, hence, appearing not resembling.
夫唯大，故，似不肖。

Identical resemble long time! His fine also man!
若肖久矣！其細也夫！

I have three treasures hold and protect him.
我有三宝持而保之。

One called humane, two called frugal, three called not dare act as all under heaven first.
一曰慈，二曰儉，三曰不敢為天下先。

Humane reason can brave, frugal reason can spread, not dare act as all under heaven first, reason can accomplish instrument to develop.
慈故能勇，儉故能广，不敢為天下先故能成器长。

Currently, abandon humane moreover brave, abandon thrifty moreover spread, abandon after further advance death!
今，舍慈且勇，舍儉且广，舍后且先死矣！

God humane, use to fight then victorious.
夫慈，以战則胜。

Use to guard strong principle. 以守則固。

<u>God will save him according to humanely defend him</u>.
天将救之以慈衛之。

The Holy Bible

For many will come in my name, claiming, '**I am the Messiah**,' and will deceive many.   Matthew 24:5

For I take no pleasure in the death of anyone, declares the Sovereign LORD. <u>Repent and live</u>!   Ezekiel 18:32

The Tao Te Ching - Chapter 68

Good act as scholar person, <u>not military</u>.
善為士者，不武。

Good war person, <u>not angry</u>. 善战者，不怒 。

Good victory, enemy person not give. 善胜，敵者不与。

Good use man, person serve as his inferior.
善用人，者為之下。

This called, not fight him virtue. 是謂，不爭之德。

This called, use person him power. 是謂，用人之力。

This means <u>blend</u> God, classic him extreme.
是謂配天，古之极。

The Holy Bible

Therefore <u>put on the full armor of God</u>, so that when the day of evil comes, you may be able to stand your ground, and after you have done everything, to stand.

Stand firm then, with the belt of truth buckled around your waist, with the breastplate of righteousness in place, and with your feet fitted with the readiness that comes from <u>the gospel of peace</u>.

In addition to all this, take up the shield of faith, with which you can extinguish all the flaming arrows of the evil one.

Take the helmet of salvation and the sword of the Spirit, which is the word of God.

And pray in the Spirit on all occasions with all kinds of prayers and requests. With this in mind, be alert and always keep on praying for all the Lord's people.   Ephesians 6:13-18

Woe unto them that call evil good, and good evil; that <u>put darkness for light, and light for darkness</u>; that put bitter for sweet, and sweet for bitter!

Woe unto them that are wise in their own eyes, and prudent in their own sight!   Isaiah 5:20-21

Jesus said, "If you were blind, you would not be guilty of sin; but now that you claim you can see, your guilt remains".
John 9:41

The Tao Te Ching - Chapter 69

<u>Use weapons, there is speech</u>. 用兵，有言。

I not dare act as host and and act as visitor.
吾不敢為主而為客。

Not dare advance an inch, but retreat a foot.
不敢進寸，而退尺。

This called, go without go. 是謂，行无行。

Take by force without arms. 攘无臂。

Throw without enemy. 扔无敵。

Execute without weapons. 执无兵。

Disaster no one great in regard to light enemy.
禍莫大于輕敵。

Light enemy how many destroy I treasure. 輕敵几吾宝。

Hence, fight soldiers mutually assist each other to increase sorrow person victory indeed.
故，抗兵相加哀者胜矣。

The Holy Bible

The tongue has the power of life and death, and those who love it will eat its fruit.   Proverbs 18:21

Everyone who believes that Jesus is the Christ is born of God, and everyone who loves the father loves his child as well.

This is how we know that we love the children of God: by loving God and carrying out his commands. In fact, this is love for God: to keep his commands. And his commands are not burdensome, for everyone born of God overcomes the world. This is the victory that has overcome the world, even our faith.

Who is it that overcomes the world? Only the one who believes that Jesus is the Son of God.   1 John 5:1-5

The Tao Te Ching - Chapter 70

I say very easy know, very easy do.
吾言甚易知,甚易行。

All under heaven none can know, none can do.
天下莫能知,莫能行。

<u>Words have purpose</u>, work to be ruler.
言有宗,事有君。

<u>Man alone without know</u>, this because I not know.
夫唯无知,是以我不知。

To know my person rare, then follow me person precious.
知我者希,則我者貴。

This according to sage man, to wear clothing think of jade.
是以圣人,被褐怀玉。

The Holy Bible

For who knows a person's thoughts except their own spirit within them?

In the same way no one knows the thoughts of God except the Spirit of God.

What we have received is not the spirit of the world, but the Spirit who is from God, so that we may understand what God has freely given us.

This is what we speak, not in words taught us by human wisdom but <u>in words taught by the Spirit, explaining spiritual realities with **Spirit-taught words**</u>.

<u>The person without the Spirit does not accept the things that come from the Spirit of God</u> but considers them foolishness, and cannot understand them because they are discerned only through the Spirit.

The person with the Spirit makes judgments about all things, but such a person is not subject to merely human judgments, for, "Who has known the mind of the Lord so as to instruct him?" But we have the mind of Christ.   1 Corinthians 2:11-16

The Tao Te Ching - Chapter 71

Understand, not know. Superior not know, <u>know disease</u>.
知，不知。 上不知，知病。

Man alone **disease defect**, that because of not fault.
夫唯病病，是以不病。

Sage man **not sick**, use his disease defect.
圣人不病，以其病病。

Man alone disease defect, <u>that because of not sick</u>.
夫唯病病，是以不病。

The Holy Bible

Therefore, just as sin entered the world through one man, and death through sin, and in this way <u>death came to all people, because all sinned</u>-- To be sure, sin was in the world before the law was given, but sin is not charged against anyone's account where there is no law.   Romans 5:12-13

Which is easier: to say, '<u>**Your sins are forgiven**</u>,' or to say, '<u>**Get up and walk**</u>'?   Matthew 9:5

As Jesus went on from there, two blind men followed him, calling out, "Have mercy on us, Son of David!" When he had gone indoors, the blind men came to him, and he asked them, "Do you believe that I am able to do this?" "Yes, Lord," they replied. Then he touched their eyes and said, "<u>According to your faith let it be done to you</u>";
                                    Matthew 9:28-29

The Tao Te Ching - Chapter 72

<u>People no fear power</u>, follow great might most.
民不畏威,則大威至。

Not be familiar with <u>his place dwell</u>. 无狎其所居。

<u>Not reject his place living</u>. 无厭其所生。

Man alone not loathe, this because not reject.
夫唯不厭,是以不厭。

That according sage man. 是以圣人。

<u>Oneself know</u>, not oneself see. 自知,不自见。

<u>Oneself love</u>, not oneself precious. 自愛,不自貴。

Reason remove that, <u>take this</u>. 故去彼,取此。

The Holy Bible

I say to you, My friends, <u>do not be afraid of those who kill the body</u> and after that have no more that they can do. "But I will warn you whom to fear: fear the One who, after He has killed, has authority to cast into hell; yes, I tell you, fear Him! Luke 12:4-5

Anyone whose name was not found written in the book of life was thrown into the <u>lake of fire</u>. Revelation 20:15

Submit therefore to God. <u>Resist the devil</u> and he will flee from you.
James 4:7

<u>For he chose us in him before the creation of the world to be holy and blameless in his sight</u>. **In love he predestined us** for adoption to sonship through Jesus Christ, in accordance with his pleasure and will-- to the praise of his glorious grace, which he has freely given us in the One he loves. Ephesians 1:4-6

If you declare with your mouth, "Jesus is Lord," and believe in your heart that God raised him from the dead, <u>you will be saved</u>.
Romans 10:9

The Tao Te Ching - Chapter 73

Brave to dare, then <u>killed</u>. 勇于敢，則殺。

Brave to not dare, then live. 勇于不敢，則活。

These both person either benefit, perhaps harm. 此兩者或利，或害。

Heaven him place hate, who know **his reason**? 天之所惡，孰知其故？

Heaven him the Way, <u>not fight</u> and good victory. 天之道，不爭而善胜。

<u>No speech</u>, yet good answer. 不言，而善應。

Not summon, yet oneself to come. 不召，而自來。

Indulgent right and good plan. 繟然而善謀。

Heaven net **to recover restore negligent**, and not to fail. 天網恢恢疏，而不失。

The Holy Bible

Indeed, all who desire to live godly in Christ Jesus <u>will be persecuted</u>. But evil men and impostors will proceed from bad to worse, deceiving and being deceived.   2 Timothy 3:12-13

Furthermore, just as **they did not think it worthwhile to retain the knowledge of God**, so God gave them over to a depraved mind, so that they do what ought not to be done. They have become filled with every kind of wickedness, evil, greed and depravity. They are full of envy, murder, strife, deceit and malice. They are gossips, slanderers, God-haters, insolent, arrogant and boastful; they invent ways of doing evil; they disobey their parents; they have no understanding, no fidelity, no love, no mercy. Although they know God's righteous decree that those who do such things deserve death, they not only continue to do these very things but also approve of those who practice them.   Romans 1:28-32

<u>Fight the good fight</u> of the faith. Take hold of the eternal life to **which you were called** when <u>you made your good confession </u>in the presence of many witnesses.   1 Timothy 6:12

Therefore we must pay much closer attention to what we have heard, lest we drift away from it. For since the message declared by angels proved to be reliable, and every transgression or disobedience received a just retribution, **how shall we escape if we neglect such a great salvation?** It was declared at first by the Lord, and it was attested to us by those who heard, while God also bore witness by signs and wonders and various miracles and by gifts of the Holy Spirit distributed according to his will.   Hebrews 2:1-4

The Tao Te Ching - Chapter 74

<u>People not fear die</u>, how use death fear him?
民不畏死，奈何以死懼之？

You cause people ordinary fear die, thus serve as strange person. 若使民常畏死，而為奇者。

<u>I need to execute these to kill him who daring</u>.
吾得执而殺之孰敢。

Constant have control to kill person <u>murder</u>. 常有司殺者殺。

Mans generation control kill person murder. 夫代司殺者殺。

That means replace great craftsman hack. 是謂代大匠斲。

Man replace great craftsman hack person, <u>hope have not injury his hands already</u>. 夫代大匠斲者，希有不傷其手矣。

The Holy Bible

<u>Do not be afraid of those who kill the body</u> but cannot kill the soul. Rather, be afraid of the One who can destroy both soul and body in hell. Matthew 10:28

Then you will be handed over to be persecuted and <u>put to death</u>, and you will be hated by all nations because of me. Matthew 24:9

And even as they did not like to retain God in their knowledge, God gave them over to a reprobate mind, to do those things which are not convenient; Being filled with all unrighteousness, fornication, wickedness, covetousness, maliciousness; full of envy, **murder**, debate, deceit, malignity; whisperers, Backbiters, haters of God, despiteful, proud, boasters, inventors of evil things, disobedient to parents, Without understanding, covenant breakers, without natural affection, implacable, unmerciful: Who knowing the judgment of God, that they which commit such things are worthy of death, not only do the same, but have pleasure in them that do them. Romans 1:28-32

But Thomas, one of the twelve, called Didymus, was not with them when Jesus came. The other disciples therefore said unto him, We have seen the Lord. But he said unto them, Except I shall <u>see in his hands the print of the nails</u>, and put my finger into the print of the nails, and thrust my hand into his side, I will not believe.

And after eight days again his disciples were within, and Thomas with them: then came Jesus, the doors being shut, and stood in the midst, and said, Peace be unto you. Then saith he to Thomas, Reach hither thy finger, and behold my hands; and reach hither thy hand, and thrust it into my side: and be not faithless, but believing. And Thomas answered and said unto him, My Lord and my God. Jesus saith unto him, Thomas, because thou hast seen me, thou hast believed: blessed are they that have not seen, and yet have believed. John 20:24-29

The Tao Te Ching - Chapter 75

<u>People they hunger</u> because his high food taxes, him more than use hunger.
民之饑以其上食稅,之多是以饑。

People him difficult control because their superior, <u>him still govern</u>. 民之難治以其上,之有為。

That because doctrine punish.
是以難治。

<u>People his light die</u> according to their request, life him generous. 民之輕死以其求,生之厚。

This because light dead. 是以輕死。

Man only nothing because life serve as person to be worthy of costly life. 夫唯无以生為者是賢于貴生。

The Holy Bible

He hath shewed strength with his arm; he hath scattered the proud in the imagination of their hearts. He hath put down the mighty from their seats, and exalted them of low degree. He hath <u>filled the hungry</u> with good things; and the rich he hath sent empty away. Luke 1:51-53

And because iniquity shall abound, the love of many shall wax cold. But <u>he that shall endure unto the end</u>, the same shall be saved. And this gospel of the kingdom shall be preached in all the world for a witness unto all nations; and then shall the end come. Matthew 24:12-14

Indeed, all who desire to live a godly life in Christ Jesus will be <u>persecuted</u>. 2 Timothy 3:12

When he opened the fifth seal, I saw under the altar the <u>souls of those who had been slain for the word of God</u> and for the witness they had borne. They cried out with a loud voice, "O Sovereign Lord, holy and true, how long before you will judge and avenge our blood on those who dwell on the earth?" Revelation 6:9-10

What then shall we say to these things? If God is for us, who can be against us?

He who did not spare his own Son but gave him up for us all, how will he not also with him graciously give us all things? Who shall bring any charge against God's elect? It is God who justifies. Who is to condemn? Christ Jesus is the one who died—more than that, who was raised—who is at the right hand of God, who indeed is interceding for us. Who shall separate us from the love of Christ? Shall tribulation, or distress, or persecution, or famine, or nakedness, or danger, or sword? Romans 8:31-35

The Tao Te Ching - Chapter 76

Man him life too <u>soft weak</u>, **his death too strong powerful.**
人之生也柔弱，其死也堅強。

<u>Careless tree</u> **him life also** also soft brittle, **his death also withered rotten.** 草木之生也柔脆，其死也枯槁。

Hence, strong powerful person <u>death these disciples</u>, soft weak person life him disciple.
故，堅強者死之徒，柔弱者生之徒。

This because <u>soldiers</u> strength rule, destroy tree power then break. 是以兵強則，滅木強則折。

Powerful great to <u>live under</u>, soft weak to <u>live above</u>.
強大処下，柔弱処上。

The Holy Bible

Blessed are <u>those who wash their robes</u>, that they may have the right to the <u>tree of life</u> and may go through the gates into the city.
Revelation 22:14

Above his head they placed the written charge against him: this is jesus, the king of the jews.
Matthew 27:37

The fruit of the righteous is a tree of life, and <u>the one who is wise saves lives</u>.
Proverbs 11:30

And the four angels were loosed, which were prepared for an hour, and a day, and a month, and a year, for to slay the third part of men. And the number of the <u>army of the horsemen</u> were two hundred thousand thousand: and I heard the number of them.
Revelation 9:15-16

Blessed are the poor in spirit, for theirs is the <u>kingdom of heaven</u>. Blessed are those who mourn, for they will be comforted. Blessed are the meek, for they will inherit the earth.

Blessed are those who hunger and thirst for righteousness, for they will be filled. Blessed are the merciful, for they will be shown mercy. Blessed are the pure in heart, for they will see God.

Blessed are the peacemakers, for they will be called children of God. Blessed are those who are persecuted because of righteousness, for theirs is the kingdom of heaven. Blessed are you when people insult you, persecute you and falsely say all kinds of evil against you because of me.

Rejoice and be glad, because great is your reward in heaven, for in the same way they persecuted the prophets who were before you.
Matthew 5:3-12

<u>Hell from beneath</u> is moved for thee to meet thee at thy coming: it stirreth up the dead for thee, even all the chief ones of the earth; it hath raised up from their thrones all the kings of the nations.
Isaiah 14:9

The Tao Te Ching - Chapter 77

<u>Heaven him the Way that still open</u>, <u>bow arched</u>.
天之道其犹張,弓与。

High person to <u>restrain</u> him, inferior person to raise him.
高者抑之,下者舉之。

Have surplus person **injure him**, not enough person **mend him**.
有余者損之,不足者補之。

God him the Way, injure collect remainder, but restore not have enough. 天之道,損有余,而补不足。

Man him the Way, follow not <u>promise</u>, injure not enough because save only remainder.
人之道,則不然,損不足以奉有余。

<u>Who can have surplus in order to receive all under heaven</u>?
孰能有余以奉天下?

Exclusively occur the Way person. 唯有道者。

This use sage man do and not rely on, merit accomplish and not rule. 是以圣人為而不恃,功成而不处。

His no desire, <u>visible virtuous evil</u>. 其不欲见賢邪。

The Holy Bible

<u>Then I saw heaven opened</u>, and behold, a white horse! The one sitting on it is called Faithful and True, and in righteousness he judges and <u>makes war</u>. Revelation 19:11

For the mystery of lawlessness is already at work; only <u>he who now restrains</u> will do so until he is taken out of the way. 2 Thessalonians 2:7

The Lord is not slow in keeping his <u>promise</u>, as some understand slowness. Instead he is patient with you, not wanting anyone to perish, but everyone to come to repentance. 2 Peter 3:9

And I stood upon the sand of the sea, and saw a beast rise up out of the sea, having seven heads and ten horns, and upon his horns ten crowns, and upon his heads the name of blasphemy. And the beast which I saw was like unto a leopard, and his feet were as the feet of a bear, and his mouth as the mouth of a lion: and the dragon gave him his power, and his seat, and great authority.

And I saw one of his heads **<u>as it were wounded to death</u>**; and **<u>his deadly wound was healed</u>**: and all the world wondered after the beast. And they worshipped the dragon which gave power unto the beast: and they worshipped the beast, saying, <u>Who is like unto the beast</u>? who is able to make war with him? Revelation 13:1-4

Evil people and impostors will become worse, <u>deceiving and being deceived</u>. 2 Timothy 3:13

The Tao Te Ching - Chapter 78

All under heaven, is not soft weak in <u>water</u>.
天下，莫柔弱于水。

Yet, attack strong powerful person is not him ability victory.
而，攻堅强者莫之能胜。

Because that, not to use change him. 以其，无以易之。

Weak him victory strong, soft him victory firm.
弱之胜强，柔之胜剛。

All under heaven can not, not know, negative energy competent. 天下莫，不知，莫能行。

<u>This use Sage man say</u>, endure country him disgrace. This called the country master.
是以圣人云，受国之垢 。 是謂社稷主。

Receiving country not have good omen, is to be all under <u>heaven king</u>. 受国不祥，是為天下王。

<u>Principle word</u> similar opposite. 正言若反。

The Holy Bible

Jesus answered her, "If you knew the gift of God and who it is that asks you for a drink, <u>you would have asked Him and He would have given you living water</u>." John 4:10

Then he showed me a river of the **water of life**, clear as crystal, coming from the throne of God and of the Lamb, in the middle of its street. On either side of the river was the tree of life, bearing twelve kinds of fruit, yielding its fruit every month; and the leaves of the tree were for the healing of the nations. Revelation 22:1-2

<u>Consult God's instruction and the testimony of warning</u>. If anyone does not speak **according to this word**, they have no light of dawn.

Distressed and hungry, they will roam through the land; when they are famished, they will become enraged and, looking upward, will curse their <u>king</u> and their God.

Then they will look toward the earth and see only distress and darkness and fearful gloom, and they will be thrust into utter darkness. Isaiah 18:20-22

The Tao Te Ching - Chapter 79

Blend great resentment, certainly have only remainder hatred.
和大怨，必有余怨。

Stoppable with <u>false good person</u>. 安可以為善。

That consider as sage man carry out improper deed, without negative responsibility toward people.
是以圣人执左契，而不責于人。

Have virtue, manage deed. 有德，司契。

Without virtue, <u>manage thorough</u>. 无德，司彻。

God the Way without love, always oppose <u>good people</u>.
天道无亲，常与善人。

The Holy Bible

Then I saw a second beast, coming out of the earth. It had two horns like a lamb, but it spoke like a dragon. It exercised all the authority of the first beast on its behalf, and made the earth and its inhabitants worship the first beast, whose fatal wound had been healed.

And it performed great signs, even causing fire to come down from heaven to the earth in full view of the people. Because of the signs it was given power to perform on behalf of the first beast, it <u>deceived the inhabitants of the earth</u>. It ordered them to set up an image in honor of the beast who was wounded by the sword and yet lived.

The second beast was given power to give breath to the image of the first beast, so that the image could speak and cause all who refused to worship the image to be killed.

<u>It also forced all people</u>, great and small, rich and poor, free and slave, to receive a mark on their right hands or on their foreheads, so that they could not buy or sell unless they had the mark, which is the name of the beast or the number of its name.

This calls for wisdom. Let the person who has insight calculate the number of the beast, for it is the number of a man. That number is 666.   Revelation 13:11-18

And Jesus said to him, Why do you call Me good? <u>No one is good except God alone</u>.   Mark 10:18

The Tao Te Ching - Chapter 80

Small country, few people. 小国寡民。

Enable have ten uncles him instruments, but not to use.
使有什伯之器，而不用。

Enable people value death, and not far migrate.
使民重死，而不遠徙。

Although have boat carriage, not have place ride it.
虽有舟輿，无所乘之。

Although have armor soldier, not have place display him.
虽有甲兵，无所陳之。

Order people repeatedly tie rope and use him.
使民复結繩而用之。

Sweet their food, beautiful their clothes, 甘其食，美其服，

quiet their dwelling, music his custom. 安其居，樂其俗。

Neighbor country mutually look towards chicken dog.
邻国相望雞犬。

They noise mutually hear. 之声相聞。

People extremely old die, not mutually go in the future.
民至老死，不相往來。

The Holy Bible

The words of the Teacher,[a] son of David, king in Jerusalem:

"Meaningless! Meaningless! says the Teacher.

"Utterly meaningless! Everything is meaningless."

What do people gain from all their labors at which they toil under the sun?

Generations come and generations go, but the earth remains forever.

The sun rises and the sun sets, and hurries back to where it rises.

The wind blows to the south and turns to the north; round and round it goes, ever returning on its course.

All streams flow into the sea, yet the sea is never full.

To the place the streams come from, there they return again.

All things are wearisome, more than one can say.

The eye never has enough of seeing, nor the ear its fill of hearing.

What has been will be again, what has been done will be done again;

there is nothing new under the sun.

Is there anything of which one can say,

    "Look! This is something new"?

It was here already, long ago; it was here before our time.

No one remembers the former generations, and even those yet to come will not be remembered by those who follow them.
                                        Ecclesiastes 1:1-11

The Tao Te Ching - Chapter 81

<u>True words not beautiful</u>. 信言不美。

Beautiful words not true. 美言不信。

Good person not argue. 善者不辯。

Argue person not good. 辯者不善。

Knowledgable person not rich. 知者不博。

Rich person not knowledgable. 博者不知。

Sage man not accumulate. 圣人不積。

Both think man self heal exists. 既以為人己愈有。

Both use together with people, self heal many.
既以与人，己愈多。

Heaven him the way benefit and not harm. 天之道利而不害。

<u>Sage man him the Way do and not fight</u>.

圣人之道為而不爭。

The Holy Bible

But godliness with contentment is great gain. For we brought nothing into the world, and we can take nothing out of it. But if we have food and clothing, we will be content with that. Those who want to get rich fall into temptation and a trap and into many foolish and harmful desires that plunge people into ruin and destruction.

For the love of money is a root of all kinds of evil. Some people, eager for money, have wandered from the faith and pierced themselves with many griefs. But you, man of God, flee from all this, and pursue righteousness, godliness, faith, love, endurance and gentleness. <u>Fight the good fight of the faith</u>.

Take hold of the eternal life to which you were called when you made your good confession in the presence of many witnesses.
1 Timothy 6:6-9

For the LORD is our judge, the LORD is our lawgiver, the LORD is our king; it is he who will save us. Isaiah 33:22

The Scientific Method

The Scientific Method

Scientific method is a way of asking and answering questions by making observations and doing experiments to obtain the truth.

The elements of scientific method are:

1) Ask a Question -- What does the 'Tao Te Ching' say?
2) Do Background Research -- Read, then talk to the experts.
3) Construct a Hypothesis -- A true translation does exist & can be obtained using reason and logic that comes from the Light of Truth.
4) Test Your Hypothesis by Doing an Experiment -- see the transcribed translation, the biblical comparison, and the illustration in this chapter.
5) Analyze Your Data and Draw a Conclusion -- Yep, I was right.
6) Communicate Your Results -- this book.

In this section, I want to show you how to obtain a literal translation for each Chinese character in the 'Tao Te Ching'. For this illustration, I've chosen to use the first verse in the 'Tao Te Ching', but you can repeat this process using any chapter or verse. Here is what you'll do:

First, decide which verse you want to obtain the literal translation for, then pick three different expert Taoist resources that provide character translations. (In the illustration on page 208-209, my sources are named under their interpreted sentences.) Each character translation from the three sources, will have some identical words, some synonyms, and some dissimilar words, or some combination thereof.

Next, you will isolate the identical words within the three translations for each character. If there are only synonyms and no identical words, look at the corresponding interpretations to see which word was used in each translator's interpretations. It's likely you will find a consensus by including the translations found in the interpretations, even if the word was not in a Word Range.

Also, Google Translate can sometimes help to narrow down a characters meaning, and thus, the word field. Of course, you will want to consider the words around the character you are working on, in order to determine which word translation is most applicable. The Light of Truth is helpful here. Knowing which dragon is the real author helps -hint, he's not a

The Scientific Method

librarian. Once you have isolated the words that are agreed upon by the three expert sources, you will officially have the literal meanings for each character. Some characters can potentially have more than one function (a conjunction, verb, noun, adverb, or an adjective), depending on its placement within a sentence. After you have created enough of a consensus translation to transcribe an entire sentence, you're ready to find the true meaning of each character in that particular sentence.

In order to obtain a sentence, you will pull one word from each character translation to place into a grammatically feasible sentence. Do not add your own words. You can only work with the words provided by the expert Chinese translators. You can use commas and periods as needed, because punctuation is rarely noted in the original texts. Once you have the most feasible sentence, you've transcribed a verse! It's that easy and you are now looking at the writing (or art work), as it was intended by its author.

Those who modify the Word Range Translation in order to contribute their thoughts to the original authors thoughts, are seeking to commandeer that authors title and prestige. They are seeking to blend their mind with the mind of the original author in order to consider themselves as "Sages" — and they do this believing that they are blending their thoughts with the mind of the wise dragon named, Liar. They do this believing that they are joining an elite class of intellectuals who are also "sages", when in reality, they are joining an epidemic of self- deluded, fallen and rebellious, individuals.
1 Corinthians 3:19 says, "For the wisdom of this world is foolishness with God. For it is written, He taketh the wise in their own craftiness."

If you've read this book, then you now know the truth, and God says: "When I say to a wicked person, 'You will surely die,' and you do not warn them or speak out to dissuade them from their evil ways in order to save their life, that wicked person will die for their sin, and I will hold you accountable for their blood (Ezekiel 3:18)".

As the author of this book, I am speaking out right now to warn those

The Scientific Method

who embrace Taoism, and the 'Tao Te Ching'. God says that if you reject truth, you will pay an eternal price. If a process of deduction can be applied to uncover a pre-existing truth (before the wisdom of human interpretation is applied to suppress that truth) — then logically the original text/ideology is intentionally deceptive! And deception is an agenda fueled by hate. Hate for God and hate for mankind.

Satan's goal is to blend man's light with his darkness just to grieve the Lord and destroy as many of God's children as he can before his time is up. Satan has already been defeated at the Cross, so now it's just a numbers game, and so many people walk around having no idea of the eternal battle raging all around them - in an effort to gain them!

There is no truth to the 'Tao Te Ching', other than what the Light has shown. The 'Tao Te Ching' is literally, nothing more than deceptive thought distracting you from reality. It's your enemy providing you with the opportunity to believe whatever you want so that you will forfeit your eternal inheritance offered to you by God.

You've been given two books (two trees) that you can eat from -- Satan's "little book of wisdom", wherein you reject God's Word and His Son in order to embrace your own thoughts and imagination (wherein you believe you are wise), or God's Book wherein you reject the sin nature to embrace God as the Way, Truth, and Life. God has given us His Word, so that when we stand before Him, no one can say, "The Serpent deceived me, and I ate" (Genesis 3:13).

Look over the following illustration (on page 208-209), and then try a sentence on your own. If you don't believe God's Word (the Bible), then believe the Power that has exposed the 'Tao Te Ching', and know that Jesus is the Son of God.

Jesus said, "Do not believe me unless I do the works of my Father. But if I do them, even though you do not believe me, believe the works, that you may know and understand that the Father is in me, and I in the Father" (John 10:38).

God Bless!

1) "The Way that can be told of is not an Unvarying Way" Tr. Waley
http://wengu.tartarie.com/wg/wengu.php?l=Daodejing&no=1

道
可 } *To suit; can; may; able to; certain(ly)*

道

非 } *Non-; not-; un-.*

常 } *Always; ever; often frequently; common; general; constant*

道

Direction; way; method; road; path; principal; truth; reason; skill; method; Tao (of Taoism). measure word; to say; speak; talk.

2) "The Dao that can be trodden is not the enduring and unchanging Dao"
http://ctext.org/dictionary.pl?if=en&id=11592

道
可 } *may; can; -able; possibly*

道

非 } *Violate, go against (a rule) Wrong, bad; Not real, untrue; Oppose, object to; Slander, condemn; Sarcasm, irony; Absence of, not have; Adverb: not, is not.*

常 } *Common; Normal; Frequent; Regular*

道

Road; path; journey; method; law; reason; doctrine; claim; skill; technique; principle; right way. Speak; talk; course of action. Rites paid to the spirit of roads. ancient administrative unit. Taoism

3) **"The way possible to think, runs counter to the constant way"**
http://www.centertao.org/tao-te-ching/carl/chapter-1/

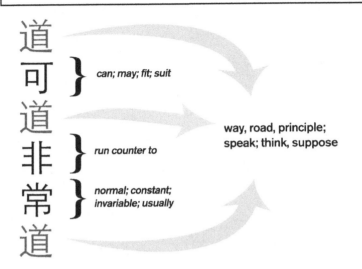

"The Way can speak, wrong constant Way"

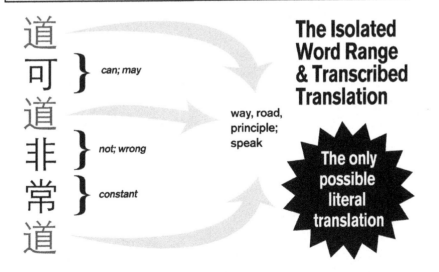

Resources and Recommended Books

Resources:

The Chinese Characters of the 'Tao Te Ching', and their translations were produced via a consensus identified in, or inspired by, the following professional sources:

(web addresses accessed as of August 20, 2015)

http://www.centertao.org/tao-te-ching/carl/

http://ctext.org/dao-de-jing#n11629

http://wengu.tartarie.comwgwengu.phpl=Daodejing&no=1

The Ma-wang-tui Text, as provided by Robert G. Henricks, in his book: "**Lao-Tzu Te-Tao Ching**, A New Translation Based on the Recently Discovered Ma-wang-tui Texts"

The Holy Bible - King James Version, Recovery Version, New International Version.

Multiple Bible translations can be found on:
http://biblehub.com/niv/genesis/1.htm

Recommended Books:

The Holy Bible - I recommend the "Recovery Version" by Living Stream Ministry (founded by Witness Lee)

In Search of Divine Reality, Science as a Source of Inspiration, By Lothar Schafer

How to Think Straight, An Introduction to Critical Reasoning, By Anthony Flew

Victorious Christian Living, By Alan Redpath

Ye SEARCH the SCRIPTURES, By Watchman Nee

Mere Christianity, By C.S. Lewis

THE END...

Made in United States
Orlando, FL
24 May 2024

47153906R00124